MYSTICAL EXPERIENCE OF GOD

Engaging contemporary discussion concerning the validity of mystical experiences of God, Jerome Gellman presents the best evidential case in favor of validity and its implications for belief in God. Gellman vigorously defends the coherence of the concept of a mystical experience of God against philosophical objections, and evaluates attempts to provide alternative explanations from sociology and neuropsychology. He then carefully examines feminist objections to male philosophers' treatments of mystical experience of God and to the traditional hierarchal concept of God. Gellman finds none of the objections decisive, and concludes that while the initial evidential case is not rationally compelling for some, it can be rationally compelling for others.

Offering important new perspectives on the evidential value of experiences of God, and the concept of God more broadly, this book will appeal to a wide range of readers including those with an interest in philosophy of religion, religious studies, mysticism and epistemology.

ASHGATE PHILOSOPHY OF RELIGION SERIES

Series Editors

Paul Helm, Emeritus Professor of the History and Philosophy of
Religion, King's College London, UK
Jerome Gellman, Ben Gurion University of the Negev, Israel
Linda Zagzebski, University of Oklahoma, USA

Due to the work of Plantinga, Alston, Swinburne and others, the philosophy
of religion is now becoming recognised once again as a mainstream
philosophical discipline in which metaphysical, epistemological and moral
concepts and arguments are applied to issues of religious belief. The *Ashgate
Philosophy of Religion Series* fosters this resurgence of interest by presenting
a number of high profile titles spanning many critical debates, and presenting
new directions and new perspectives in contemporary research and study.
This new series presents books by leading international scholars in the field,
providing a platform for their own particular research focus to be presented
within a wider contextual framework. Offering accessible, stimulating new
contributions to each topic, this series will prove of particular value and
interest to academics, graduate, postgraduate and upper-level undergraduate
readers world-wide focusing on philosophy, religious studies and theology,
sociology or other related fields.

Mystical Experience of God
A Philosophical Inquiry

JEROME GELLMAN
Ben-Gurion University of the Negev, Israel

Aldershot • Burlington USA • Singapore • Sydney

Published by
Ashgate Publishing Limited
Gower House
Croft Road
Aldershot
Hants GU11 3HR
England

Ashgate Publishing Company
131 Main Street
Burlington VT 05401-5600 USA

Ashgate website: http://www.ashgate.com

British Library Cataloguing in Publication Data
Gellman, Jerome I.
   Mystical experience of God : a philosophical inquiry. -
   (Ashgate philosophy of religion series)
   1. God - Knowableness - Philosophy 2. Experience (Religion)
   3. Mysticism
   I.Title
   231.7'4'01

Library of Congress Cataloging-in-Publication Data
Gellman, Jerome I.
   Mystical experience of God : a philosophical inquiry / Jerome Gellman.
      p. cm. -- (Ashgate philosophy of religion series)
   Includes bibliographical references.
   ISBN 0-7546-1443-3 -- ISBN 0-7546-1445-X (pbk.)
   1. Mysticism. 2. Experience (Religion) 3. Knowledge, Theory of (Religion) 4.
God--Proof, Empirical. I. Title. II. Series.

   BL625.G44 2001
   291.4'22'01--dc21

                                                          2001032800

ISBN 0 7546 1443 3 (Hbk)
ISBN 0 7546 1445 X (Pbk)

Typeset by Manton Typesetters, Louth, Lincolnshire, UK and printed and bound in Great Britain by MPG Books Ltd., Bodmin, Cornwall.

In memory of
Blumah Enkah

And in Hope
to
Chana Gila and Binyamin
Yael Rena and Aharon Meir
Menachem and Yonah
Uriel and Shira
Aviezer and Shlomit
Ditza
Yechiel
and
Yedidia

Contents

Acknowledgements

Curzon Press has granted permission to reproduce material in Chapter Three from my article, 'Identifying God in Experience: On Strawson, Sounds and God's Space' in Paul Helm (ed.), *Referring to God, Jewish and Christian Philosophical and Theological Perspectives*, Richmond, Surrey: Curzon, 2000, pp. 71–89.

Parts of Chapter Five appeared in my article, 'On a sociological challenge to the veridicality of religious experience', *Religious Studies*, **34**, pp. 235–51 (1998).

I am thankful to many people who gave me valuable assistance at various stages of the preparation of this book. I wish to thank especially Pamela Anderson, Alex Blum, Sarah Coakley, Evan Fales, Muhammad Hourani, Richard Gale, Yakir Levine, Yuval Lurie, Chana Safrai, David Shatz, Ira Schnall, Phillip Wexler and David Widerker.

This work was completed at the Robert P. and Arlene R. Kogod Institute for Advanced Judaic Studies of the Shalom Hartman Institute in Jerusalem, where I am a Fellow, while on sabbatical from Ben-Gurion University of the Negev. I thank David Hartman, the Director, as well as the staff and fellows of the Institute for providing an optimal atmosphere for scholarly endeavor.

JG

Chapter 1

Introduction

I began to think of the soul as if it were a castle made of a single diamond or of very clear crystal, in which there are many rooms, just as in Heaven there are many mansions ... Let us now imagine that this castle, as I have said, contains many mansions, some above, others below, others at each side; and in the centre and midst of them all is the chiefest mansion where the most secret things pass between God and the soul.

Teresa of Avila (1961), 'First Mansion', Chapter One

This book is about mystical experiences of God. Specifically it is an epistemological inquiry into whether people have had valid, reliable experiential contact with God. Various philosophers have been sympathetic to the idea that people do genuinely know God through mystical experience.[1]

Richard Swinburne writes, 'I suggest that the overwhelming testimony of so many millions of people to occasional experiences of God must, in the absence of counter-evidence of the kind analyzed, be taken as tipping the balance of evidence decisively in favour of the existence of God' (Swinburne, 1996, p. 138). Swinburne believes that mystical experiences of God give evidence that God is in real contact with human beings. He also believes that when this evidence is added to other evidence we can obtain a cumulative evidential case for God's existence.

Keith Yandell endorses what he calls an 'evidential argument' that begins with the premise that 'experiences occur which are a matter of their subjects at least seeming to experience God' and concludes from this, together with auxiliary premises, that 'These experiences give them evidence that God exists.' He then concludes further that people who have not had such experiences can rely on the evidence to conclude that God exists (Yandell, 1999, pp. 231 and 234–5).

More cautiously, William Wainwright characterizes his study of mystical experiences, including mystical experiences of God, as showing that 'there are good, if not conclusive reasons, for believing that some mystical experiences are veridical, and that the claims which are built into them are true' (Wainwright, 1981, pp. xiv–xv).

In a previous work I have defended the rationality of recognizing the validity of at least some mystical experiences of God (Gellman, 1997). I defended a line of reasoning starting from mystical experiences of God as a widely occurring phenomenon to the conclusion that some people through

1

experience really knew God. While this line of reasoning is not universally rationally compelling, in that not everyone would be required to agree with its conclusion, I argued that many would be justified in finding it rationally compelling for them.[2]

Other philosophers have disagreed.[3] After finding what he considers serious difficulties with the evidential merit of mystical theistic experiences, Evan Fales concludes that: 'Until these defects are remedied, mystical experience cannot hope to provide significant evidential support for theism' (Fales, 2001).

Richard Gale argues vigorously against mystical experiences of God having any evidential value whatsoever, declaring that '... a religious experience ... could not qualify as a veridical perception of an objective reality, even if its apparent object were to exist and be the cause of the experience' (Gale, 1995, p. 287). And Michael Martin concludes a lengthy critical examination of claimed experiences of God with the blunt, 'Religious experiences provide no evidence for the existence of God' (Martin, 1990, p. 186).

William Rowe has considered what he takes to be the main way of arguing from mystical experiences of God to God's existence and concludes that the argument is defective and, therefore, fails to show that it is probable that God exists (Rowe, 1982).

In this book I hope to contribute beyond my earlier work toward the clarification and resolution of some of the fundamental issues in this philosophical debate. Since my earlier treatment of the topic, firstly I have had to rethink the case in favor of the validity of mystical experiences of God. Secondly, I have come upon new, challenging objections to the validity of experiences of God, which demand careful consideration. Thirdly, I have come to better appreciate the serious potential of alternative, naturalistic explanations of mystical experiences of God. Fourthly, I recognize the importance of a variety of feminist critiques of the enterprise in which I am engaged.

Accordingly, the game plan of the present inquiry is to begin by presenting what I take now to be the best case for the validity of (at least some) mystical experiences of God. I then will follow with an examination of important challenges to that initial case, including a cluster of proposals of naturalistic explanations of such experiences. My purpose will be to assess the strength of the challenges against the initial rationale in favor of the validity of mystical experiences of God.

I caution against thinking of this work as simply equivalent to an attempt to prove God's existence. To be sure, that people have genuine, valid experiences of God entails that God exists. As we have seen, some philosophers have wanted to infer God's existence from an argument for the authenticity of God-perceptions. Yet the question whether people ever genuinely experience God is not necessarily equivalent to the question whether God exists, any more than my asking whether you have ever visited Jerusalem need imply my wondering whether Jerusalem exists. On the one hand, my topic will interest those who wish to know whether the phenomenon of mystical experiences of God confirms or supports the existence of God. On the other hand, the topic need not be approached in that spirit. A theist may ask the question this book addresses without God's existence being at stake. The evidential value of God-experiences might be an open question for that theist. So asking whether there are genuine experiences of God need not imply wondering whether God exists.

It would be a mistake to think that a discussion of the epistemic value of mystical experiences of God must start by pretending we have no other reason for thinking God exists. That we have other reasons is a respectable, widely-held philosophical position, so a discussion of whether God is genuinely experienced can be fruitfully conducted along those lines just as well as on the other lines.

Furthermore, the epistemic situation, for the justified theist is not the same as for the non-theist. If one is rationally warranted in believing that God exists before an examination of mystical experiences of God, it will be epistemically easier to justify believing that people genuinely experience God than it would be otherwise. If God exists, it is quite plausible to think God would become experientially available in some way or other to human beings. This consideration provides support for the genuineness of experience of God. In what follows, therefore, we should keep in mind the epistemic disparity that could arise for justified theists and others, respectively, when weighing the evidential force of mystical experiences of God.

Mystical Experiences of God

Mystical experiences of God come in varied forms. Some occur suddenly and pass quickly, while others involve an ongoing sense of God's presence in one's life. Some experiences arise in prayer and contemplation, as for Teresa of Avila, while others come at unexpected times or circumstances. Some are quite dramatic and emotionally arousing, while others are quieting and peaceful. Some experiences are rich in content, while others are said to be mysteriously devoid of positive content. With all their differences, these experiences have in common the inclination of subjects to think that they had come into genuine experiential contact with God.

The terms 'mysticism' and 'mystical experience' enjoy a notoriously wide range of meanings, or lack of clear meaning. These terms can denote, depending on the speaker, anything from a philosophical system positing unseen, mysterious objects, to an ideology thought (by those who do not give it credence) to be baseless for lacking grounding in empirical facts and scientific investigation. In 1899, W.R. Inge listed 26 different definitions of 'mysticism' (Inge, 1899). The famous scholar of mysticism, Evelyn Underhill (1945, p. 72), wrote that 'mysticism' which is applied to the performance of mediums and the ecstasies of saints, to 'menticulture' and sorcery, dreamy poetry and mediaeval art, to prayer and palmistry, the doctrinal excesses of Gnosticism, and the tepid speculations of Cambridge Platonists – even, according to William James, to the higher branches of intoxication – soon ceases to have any useful meaning.

When scholars turn to defining 'mysticism' and 'mystical experience', the results differ greatly. William James defined a mystical experience as one marked by 'ineffability' (not given to linguistic expression), a 'noetic quality' (thought to convey knowledge), transience and passivity (James, 1958, pp. 370–72). In contrast, Underhill defined 'mysticism' as an active life-process of the 'whole self', aimed at the 'changeless One', which is a loving and personal object of love, culminating in union with the One in a 'unitive state' (Underhill, 1945, p. 81). The *Catholic Encyclopedia* states that mysticism is 'either a religious tendency and desire of the human soul towards an intimate union with the Divinity, or a system growing out of such a tendency and desire'. Further, mysticism involves 'the direct union of the human soul with the Divinity through contemplation and love. This contemplation ... is not based on a merely analogical knowledge of the Infinite, but [is] a direct and immediate intuition of the Infinite'.

Recently, Robert Elwood (1999, p. 39) defined 'mystical experience' as

Experience in a religious context that is immediately or subsequently interpreted by the experiencer as a direct, unmediated encounter with ultimate divine reality. This experience engenders a deep sense of unity and suggests that during the experience the experiencer was living on a level of being other than the ordinary.

In light of this variety, rather than fuss over what 'mysticism' and 'mystical experience' 'really' mean or 'should' mean, I prefer simply to stipulate what these terms shall mean for the purposes of the present study.

Accordingly, by a 'mystical experience' I shall mean an experience in which a person allegedly has a nonsensory perception apparently of a reality (or state of affairs) of a sort that can neither be perceived by sense perception nor known by ordinary introspective self-awareness. Typically, I imagine, when having mystical experiences subjects not only are in such perceptual states but also *take themselves* to be in perceptual contact with a supersensory reality.[4]

Explaining further the components of this characterization, a mystical experience is a 'perception' in the sense of including a phenomenal content present to the subject as an alleged appearance of a reality or state of affairs. The phenomenal content possesses a subject-object structure. That is, the experience includes the sense of something being present to the subject. Mystical experiences sometimes involve heightened affective states and sometimes entail unusual behavior or speech. However, I do not identify the mystical experience with these. In mystical experience, the ground of the emotional state of the subject and of the accompanying behavior is a perception by the subject. When children see their toys, they may become quite excited and run toward the toys. A good description of what had taken place would not be one that refers only to the heightened emotional state of the child and to the running. Rather, children had perceived what they took to be their toys, and so were excited and ran to them. In the same way, we are to regard mystical experiences as perceptions with a phenomenal content of an alleged reality or state of affairs, accompanied by various affective states and behaviors.

To say that mystical experience is an allegedly 'nonsensory' perception means that the perception is supposed to be neither via the five senses nor by way of one's inner sense of what is happening with or in one's body. This is what Hildegarde of Bingen (1098–1179) called 'the eyes of the spirit and the inner ear' (see Borchert 1994, p. 56). The idea is that there is an additional nonsensory, 'mystical sense' by which people can perceive phenomenal content of a different sort than that available by the ordinary sensory means. Because nonsensory, we are to think of the mystical component of mystical experience *per se* as excluding sensory content, such as visual or auditory images.

This is not to assert that sense perceptions cannot accompany mystical experiences. In this connection we should distinguish between those mystical experiences in which the subject loses all sense awareness, including awareness of the body and even of the 'self', and those in which the subject is aware of self and has sense experiences. The latter can be subdivided into at least three categories: the first is when the sense perception is merely the occasion for a mystical episode. This can happen, for example, when a person gazes at a sunset and suddenly becomes aware of a mystical reality 'behind' the sun, as it were. The second occurs when the mystical reality is perceived somehow 'inside' the occurring sense content. A poet, for example, might 'hold infinity' in the palm of his hand (Blake, 'Auguries of Innocence').

The third kind of sense experience accompanying mystical experience is when extraordinary sensory input occurs along with the mystical perception. Sometimes, people having mystical experiences report seeing light or hearing sounds, for example. We might want to interpret some light-and-sound mysticism as a nonsensory analogue to physical light and sound, as probably in the following description: 'With that I was immersed in a sweetness words cannot express. I could hear the singing of the planets, and wave after wave of light washed over me. But this is wrong, because I *was* the light as well, without distinction of self or being washed' (Burnham, 1997, pp. 78–9, as quoted in Wulff, 2000, p. 398). At other times, though, people seem to sense unusual light that appears to them as a physical reality. The latter cases would be examples of out of the ordinary sensory input accompanying mystical experiences. In such cases what makes the episode 'mystical', in my sense, is not the mysterious sensory apparition, but the nonsensory perception occurring at the same time.[5]

I say a person in a mystical experience has an experience 'apparently' of a reality or state of affairs. 'Apparently' because, in order to agree that mystical experiences occur, we need not agree there actually exists a reality or state of affairs known by the perceiving subject. In addition, when we do agree the reality exists, we need not admit the subject genuinely knows it in experience. A subject may be mistaken in thinking the perception is veridical. We want to recognize the existence of mystical experiences and leave open whether what seems to be perceived really exists. Therefore, in my characterization, I allow no more than that there *seems* to be an object of the perceptual experience.

A subject, I say, seems to perceive a 'reality or state of affairs'. The reality might be, for example, God, Brahman, or the ultimate ground of all being. The 'state of affairs' might be the 'unity of all beings' or 'nothingness', for example. Experiences of 'nothingness' are recounted in mystical literature, though it is not (always) clear whether nothingness is a kind of reality or the absence of all reality, or yet something else.[6] I call nothingness and other hard-to-classify 'objects' of mystical experiences 'states of affairs' as a catch-all term to include whatever is thought to be revealed to the subject that we may not want to call a 'reality'.

Next, I said that the alleged reality or state of affairs could neither be perceived by sense perception nor known by ordinary introspective self-awareness. This points to the nature of the entities thought to be mystically accessible. This clause excludes a range of anomalous experiences I do not wish to include in the term 'mystical experience'. The anomalous experiences I wish to exclude take in 'synesthesia' where sense modalities are crossed (as when a taste seems yellow), out of body experiences, so-called 'psi-related experiences', including telepathy (mind to mind communication), precognition ('seeing' the future), clairvoyance ('seeing' distant events), and psychokinesis (thoughts causing physical events directly), and past-life and near-death experiences.[7] These anomalous experiences get left out because either they do not involve nonsensory perceptual content (as in psychokinesis, for instance) or they involve the perception solely of objects or qualities perceivable by the senses (as in clairvoyance, for example) or by introspection (as in telepathy). Although one person cannot know the thoughts of another, nonetheless telepathy involves the perception of thoughts, a category available to introspection. I am assuming that God, Brahman, and the Oneness of all reality cannot be accessed (literally) by sense perception or by ordinary introspection. On the other hand, if a subject looking deeply inward in contemplation accesses a mystical object, this does not involve 'ordinary' introspection.

If a person perceives in a nonsensory way either God or the unity of all reality or the void at the heart of all being we have a mystical experience. If a person were to come to perceive the All by a deep meditative introspection, that too would count as a mystical experience in my terminology. On the other hand, if a person were to 'see' today that tomorrow it would rain (sees, in the mind's eye, tomorrow's rain), that would not be a mystical experience. Tomorrow's rain may not be accessible to the senses today, but is in principle accessible to the senses tomorrow.

I am also excluding sensory experiences that we might want to call 'experiences of God' but which I do not include under the rubric 'mystical experience'. Here is an example. Suppose the sky all over the world became a fiery red. At every point on earth, the sky then seemed to open and wondrous colors and shapes poured out. A mighty voice booms in the language of every person on earth: 'I am the Lord your God, the God of traditional theism.' The sick are healed and the lame walk. Each person discovers great love and wholeness within. The voice goes on to explain in simple terms the reason for the evil in the world, and every person finds this rationally compelling. It snows at the equator and barren trees produce lovely fruit and wondrous flowers in abundance. The lion lies down with the lamb.[8] Although such events might count as an 'experience of God', they would not include nonsensory perception of God.[9] That's because they would not involve a nonsensory, phenomenal presentation of God. Therefore, they do not count in my category of mystical experience. I make a distinction, therefore, between an 'experience of God' and a 'mystical experience of God'. Although every instance of the latter is an instance of the former, the reverse is not true.[10]

My reason for restricting the term 'mystical experience' to the perception of realities not available to the physical senses is two-fold. Firstly, the seeing of unusual visions and hearing unusual voices, mimicking sense perception, characterizes not only some 'spiritual' perceptions, but also various forms of mental illness. For that reason there likely would be a natural resistance to taking these as indications of an experience of an objective reality. I prefer, therefore, to exclude such manner of experience from the mystical in order to present the best case for the genuineness of mystical experiences of God. Secondly, important mystics have demoted the value of unusual visions and voices to their meeting God, on the grounds that these do not afford a deep sense of God's presence. Thus Bernard of Clairvaux distinguishes between an 'inner' vision that is not sensory, and an 'external' one that is (quoted in Jantzen, 1989, p. 304):

> It is beyond question that the vision is all the more delightful the more inward it is, and not external. It is the Word, who penetrates without sound; who is effective though not pronounced, who wins the affection without striking on the ears. His face, though without form, is the source of form, it does not dazzle the eyes of the body but gladdens the watchful heart.

A corporeal image could not be God, since God is spiritual. Grace Jantzen has found similar sentiments in Julian of Norwich (Jantzen, 1989, pp. 308–13). I therefore find it appropriate to focus on perceptions of realities that cannot be perceived by the senses as representing the important realm of the mystical.

A mystical experience 'of God' is one in which the alleged object is God. In this book I will call something a 'perception of God' or a 'God-perception' or a 'mystical experience of God' if it *seems* to be an 'of-God' experience, whether genuine or not. So in my terminology, that people have a perception or a mystical experience of God does not in itself mean they are in genuine contact with God. It may only appear that way. When I want to refer to a perceptual episode as really, and not only seemingly, of God, one in which God really is perceived, I will talk of 'real', 'valid', 'veridical', 'genuine' or 'authentic' perception, mystical experience and contact with God.

God

'God' has many and varied meanings. In this study we need attend to only realist conceptions of God. A 'realist' conception of God takes 'God' to be a referring term, that is a term intended to refer to an existing reality (whether it actually exists or not). A non-realist conception of God takes 'God' not to be a referring term but as serving other linguistic tasks. These might include 'God' being part of a discourse through which one expresses an attitude toward the world or reinforces moral behavior.[11] Only a realist concept of God interests us here since we are investigating whether mystical experiences provide evidence for the existence of God as their experiential object.

At one end of the range of concepts of God we have that of the dominant Western theological tradition. In that tradition 'God' names the eternal, all-powerful, all-knowing, and perfectly good, creator and sustainer of the universe. Call this the 'classic' conception of God. At the other end of the range we have what I would call a 'generic' concept of God. In the generic sense, 'God' names a reality, the mystical perception of which holds great meaning and value for subjects, and around which – God and the experiences – subjects find the focus and integration of their lives. The generic concept leaves quite open just what descriptive attributes this reality might possess. Robert Nozick has a concept of God quite similar to the generic concept. To Nozick, 'God' names a reality that, firstly, is more intrinsically valuable than any other actual (not necessarily any other possible) reality; secondly, is exceedingly high on the scale of value, thirdly, possesses value vastly greater than that of any other actual reality; and, fourthly, is one upon which all other realities (at least all contingent ones) are dependent in some important ways (Nozick, 1989, pp. 46–54).

On both conceptions, and on any other appropriate to this study, we are to think of God as a self-initiating reality, whether literally or in some figurative or analogical sense. In some important sense, that is, we are to think of God actively appearing to people, granting a glimpse of God, as it were, rather than people simply stumbling upon God or undertaking a regimen that simply must culminate in God's being revealed to them, whether God 'wishes to' or not. This, I suggest, is part of what it means for people to experience God as a 'personal' reality.

I do not rule out the possibility that people could have phenomenal experiences of God as classically conceived, and there are reports of mystical experiences of that kind. However, much of the literature of reported mystical experiences of God appears to involve far less phenomenally than the God of Western theology. William Alston has made the point as follows (1991, p. 293):

> Frequently what is explicitly presented in putative experience of God fails to uniquely identify the object as God. One is aware of God's being *very* loving and powerful but not infinitely loving and powerful. One is aware of something sustaining one in being, but not aware of it as the creator of all.

Many experiences are even 'thinner' than Alston's example. Here is an example of a thinner experience in a report given by a British geography student: '... last week, I was walking along, when looking over the valley, I got this strange feeling. I suddenly went cold and hot again. My mind turned to thoughts about what life is all about and I felt I was not alone' (Hay, 1979, as cited in Hardy, 1980, p. 148). This student proceeded to refer to this as an awareness of the presence of God.

Thin mystical experiences might be enough to count as perceptions of God according to the generic concept. If anything like the classical God-concept is on the agenda, however, more will be needed. Alston maintains that the identification of God as the object of experience, under the classical concept, happens within what he calls a 'doxastic practice'.[12] Roughly, a doxastic practice involves a socially recognized practice of forming certain kinds of beliefs based on particular kinds of cognitive input, together with background beliefs relevant to the subject matter. For example, the doxastic practice of forming physical object beliefs from sense perception forms perceptual beliefs based on sensory input, together with our background beliefs about the physical world. So, if you see no more than a solitary branch protruding from behind a house, you take an entire tree to be standing on the other side of the house, your belief generated by your perception plus your background beliefs about the physical world.

Similarly, Alston maintains that in the 'Christian mystical practice' subjects make identifications of God based on their perceptions together with the background of Christian teachings about God. The Christian background, then, will supply the elements of God's classical attributes not available phenomenally. Alston focuses on justifying people's engaging in mystical doxastic practices like the Christian one. My focus, on the other hand, is on judging the entire phenomenon of mystical experiences of God across religions, and outside of them as well. For my purposes, then, we would have to think of identifying God as the object of mystical experience on grounds

wider than any local doxastic practice and independently of any particular
religious tradition.

Our inquiry, then, will have to start on a phenomenal conception of God
from close-up to the experiences themselves. Our source will be the known
accumulation of alleged God-sightings by people in various religions and
cultures over time. These will provide both perceptual content and a certain
experiential 'flavor'. The perceptual content will include both positive content as well as what is claimed to be the experience of God's mystery or
'unknowedness'. The 'flavor' will include the impact of the perception upon
subjects, the emotional response thought appropriate to it, and an experiential 'flavoring' not quite perceptual in nature. In surveying God-perceptions,
we must make an effort to recover types of mystical experiences that have
been suppressed or neglected. These include women's experiences of God.
Adding to the reservoir of reports in this way will enrich our understanding
of the phenomenology of God-perceptions.

The accumulation of reports of experiences over time will provide a
family of perceptions and flavors that seem to belong together, (presumably) pointing to God as object. (Problem: Might not the apparent phenomenal diversity in mystical experiences of God make it impossible to pool
such experiences together to form even a family of perceptions? Why suppose, even if we assume they have a real object, that they are perceptions of
one object rather than of a diversity of objects? I touch on this problem in
the following chapter and in a more basic way in Chapter Three.)

It is questionable whether on a phenomenal basis alone the family of
mystical experiences of God would strongly support the classical concept of
God. To get the latter, we would have to relate God-perceptions to the body
of teachings of mystical traditions in the developed Western religions or to
their theological traditions. There is an impressive over-all phenomenal
similarity with regard to the idea of God in these traditions, despite obvious
discrepancies in details.[13] We would take the intersection of those traditions
as a kind of wider theory in which thin mystical experiences of God get
placed. I leave it an open question whether such an interpretive framework
is justified, and resolve to include both the classical and generic God-
concepts in this study. Consequently, unless otherwise noted, in what follows I intend for either the classical or generic meanings to be plugged in
for the term 'God' and to serve to unpack the meaning of the term 'theism'.

Outline of the Chapters

Chapter Two: 'The Arguments from Perception'

Chapter Two develops the initial case for thinking God comes into real experiential contact with people in mystical experiences. I begin with a version
of the argument I defended in the past. The Argument from Perception calls

our attention to mystical experiences of God having a perceptual quality. In such episodes, that is, subjects seem to be confronted with an object or reality that appears to or is present to them in a nonsensory way. When having such an experience, a person experiences some perceptual content (purportedly) representing God or God's presence. Consequently, we should relate to the validity of mystical God-experiences as we would to the validity of any other type of perceptual claim. With regard to other perceptual claims, particularly about physical objects, we take a perceptual episode as evidence for its own validity until we have reason to think otherwise. Hence this version of the Argument from Perception concludes that we should be taking mystical experiences of God as evidence for their validity until shown otherwise. There may be reasons against being convinced by this evidence, but until such reasons are found we have in the perceptual nature of mystical experiences of God at least an initial case for their validity.

I go on to show how this version of the Argument from Perception is vulnerable to criticism because it depends on 'strong-foundationalism', a view controversial among epistemologists. Strong-foundationalism might give too much epistemic advantage to individual perceptual episodes. Therefore, I proceed to reformulate the argument in 'weak-foundationalist' terms, that weaken the power of individual perceptions, and intimate how it could be formulated as well in other epistemologies. I contend that a revised Argument from Perception provides good initial evidence for the validity of mystical experiences of God.

I close Chapter Two with a brief summary of my replies, from my earlier work, to a number of objections against the validity of mystical experiences of God. Firstly, a great number of people are never graced with mystical experiences of God. Their failure to perceive God should count against the validity of such experiences. Secondly, there is no way to discover that a mystical experience of God is delusory. Whatever a subject says goes. However, if there is no way to show that an experience is delusory, it cannot be positive evidence for its genuineness. Hence mystical experiences of God cannot count toward their own genuineness. Thirdly, there is the existence of specific proposals of naturalistic explanations of mystical experiences of God, superior to the theistic account, namely that God was truly experienced. And, fourthly, the diversity of religious experiences across religions and cultures prohibits taking any one type of experience as more valid than any other type.

After Chapter Two, the remainder of this book consists of detailed discussions of three broad lines of objection to the Argument from Perception. These are: firstly, an objection centered on the 'non-dimensionality' of God, that is on God's not existing in both space and time; secondly, important attempts at naturalistic explanations for mystical experiences of God (that I have not previously considered), explanations deemed superior to the theistic understanding; and thirdly, gender objections to the epistemological enterprise of evaluating the validity of mystical experiences of God.

Chapter Three: God's Non-dimensionality and Mystical Experience of God

Chapter Three, the most technical chapter of the book, concentrates on the implications of the non-dimensionality of God for the possibility of valid God-perceptions. Richard Gale has argued vigorously that mystical experiences cannot count as evidence for God's existence because of metaphysical and epistemological problems with identifying God as the object of those experiences (1994, 1995). Gale argues that God could be an object of a mystical experience only if possessed of 'dimensionality', that is of the dimensions of both time and space, or something analogous to them. However, God lacks dimensionality, so cannot be the object of a mystical experience.

According to this objection, whenever one can be said to perceive a particular object there must be a way, in principle at least, to distinguish conceptually and epistemically between two possibilities. The first possibility is that one indeed perceives the object in question; the other is that one perceives a different object phenomenally indistinct (for the moment at least) from the one in question. For example, in order for me to be justified in saying I see my pen, in principle there must be a way to distinguish between my seeing my pen and my seeing something else, that appears to me in a way indistinguishable from the way my pen appears to me. In the case of physical objects, as with my pen, the in-principle way of distinguishing between the two possibilities is to place them within the grid of spatial-temporal relations between objects. My pen will have spatial and temporal relations with other objects, in the past and present, that something else that is not my pen will lack, not withstanding their similarity in appearance. If there were no way to make this distinction, there would be no way to relate appearances to particular objects. God lacks dimensionality, so we cannot identify God in a perception-like experience, according to Gale. I will argue that God's lack of dimensionality does not damage the possibility of valid, justified mystical perceptions of God. Because of the relative technicality of this chapter, some readers may be interested in reading the other chapters first. Doing so will not impair understanding of their reading.

Chapter Four: Alternative Explanations I: The Alternative Explanation Response

Chapters Four and Five are devoted to the topic of alternative, naturalistic explanations of mystical experiences of God. Chapter 4 distinguishes two types of 'reductionist' approaches. The first proposes naturalistic conditions believed to explain God-perceptions better than does the claim that subjects really know God by experience. Under this heading I distinguish between explanations that wish to conclude that subjects do not ever experience God, that mystical experiences are delusory, and explanations that argue only that whether or not God is genuinely experienced we have no good evidence to that effect. I show what it would take for either form of reductionism to be successful.

The second approach I call the 'disappearance theory'. It argues that we would have to admit to their being some naturalistic explanation or other for mystical experiences of God even were we to lack a plausible actual candidate for explanation. This follows from our commitment to scientific explanation. Hence in principle God should 'disappear' from our explanations of mystical experiences altogether. Under this heading I examine the broadly critical stand of Matthew Bagger, who intends to build on motifs of Wittgenstein and Richard Rorty to reject the category of supernatural explanation as a way of explaining events in the world (Bagger, 1999). Since a theistic understanding of mystical experiences of God entails a supernatural explanation of particular events, we should, according to this, shun the theistic understanding. I argue that Bagger's blitz shows only that the Argument from Perception is not universally rationally compelling, but does not show that it cannot be rationally compelling for many.

Chapter Five: Alternative Explanations II: Sociological and Neuropsychological Proposals

In Chapter Five I deal with three specific alternative-explanation proposals, one sociological and two neuropsychological. I begin with a sociological explanation of mystical experiences of God offered by Evan Fales (1996a and 1996b). Fales extends to theistic mysticism a theory of the anthropologist I. Lewis about spirit-possession. Lewis explains spirit-possession in terms of the social and material advantages to the possessed person. Similarly, Fales tries to explain theistic experiences in terms of the social and political power they grant the mystic and the mystic's favored group. I will argue against Fales on both empirical and philosophical grounds. On empirical grounds I offer several counterexamples to Fales' thesis from the history of mysticism and from the phenomenon of 'normal mysticism'. Philosophically I question whether Lewis' theory about spirit-possession is well transferred to mystical experiences of God.

I then go on to consider a neuropsychological explanation from C. Daniel Batson, Patricia Schoenrade and W. Larry Ventis (1993). The 'analogical explanation' constructs an analogy between the neuropsychology of creative problem-solving and mystical experiences. Batson et al. endorse a psychological analysis of creative problem solving due to Graham Wallas that they apply to mystical experience. They wed this analogy to a hemispheric theory of brain activity in both creative problem solving and mystical experience to subsume mystical experiences under a neuropsychological explanation. I argue that the analogical form of neuropsychological explanation falls short of being a good explanation for a large class of mystical experiences of God.

Finally, I consider a neuropsychological theory of mystical experience that has attracted quite a bit of attention, that of Eugene d'Aquili and

Andrew Newberg (see d'Aquili and Newberg, 1993, 1999 and 2000). This theory proposes understanding mystical states as resulting from 'deafferentiation' or the cutting off of neural input into various structures of the nervous system. By distinguishing different forms of deafferentiation and their possible effects, the authors explain both theistic and nontheistic experiences and place mystical experiences on a neuropsychological continuum with other types of experiences, such as the aesthetic. This theory has strong theoretical power and is in all likelihood the most promising neuropsychological theory to have come along. I point out some defects in this neuropsychological theory, but my main interest is to explore what it would take for a theory of this type to impugn the initial case for the validity of mystical experiences of God. I conclude that while there may yet be no quite adequate neuropsychological explanation, this type of theory poses a most serious potential threat to the theistic understanding of God-experiences.

Chapter Six: Gender and Mystical Experience of God

Chapter Six focuses on gender issues and the epistemology of mystical experiences of God. Male philosophers of religion, particularly of an analytic orientation, have too long ignored or under-appreciated the importance of feminist thinking and its implications for philosophy of religion. (A notable exception is Peter Byrne, 1995.) The topics involved deserve more attention than I can give them in a work of this sort, but attention they deserve. I hope my relatively brief discussion of gender and mystical experiences of God will help further an interaction between feminist thought and analytic philosophy of religion.

In this chapter I take up three quite different feminist challenges: a moral objection, an epistemological objection, and a theological objection.

The moral objection comes from the important work of Grace Jantzen, who has contended that the treatment by male philosophers of religion of mystical experience reinforces the evils of patriarchal oppression (1995). It does this both by relegating women to the sphere of the 'private' as well as by neglecting questions of justice regarding the history of mystical experience. I argue that an inquiry such as that undertaken in this book need not relegate women to the private sphere, in any sinister sense, nor perpetrate any other injustice again.

The epistemological objection comes from the view that concepts of 'experience', 'evidence', 'rationality' and the like, so central to the inquiry, run the danger of reflecting androcentric biases that tend to exclude women from recognized discourse. My discussion agrees with the need to be on guard for this danger, and appeals to 'standpoint epistemology' as help toward correcting androcentric biases.

The theological objection makes the deepest challenge to analytic philosophy of religion by repudiating the classic concept of God so usual to its discourse. I, too, countenance the classical concept of God, so the feminist critique of the classical concept as representing males' wildest dreams for themselves, and thus a source of male abuse, sticks to me as well. I argue in reply that we need repudiate the classical concept of God in the name of justice only if we uphold a religious ideal of an unrestricted imitation of God. I argue that a just theology can be achieved with the classical concept of God if we either restrict the concept of *imitatio dei* or de-emphasize it altogether. First I expound a tradition-friendly, restricted version of *imitatio dei* based on a modification of the thought of Maimonides. I follow this with a more radical departure from tradition with an alternative that de-emphasizes the imitation of God in favor of what I call a 'non-imitative theology'. I contend that a non-imitative theology has what it takes to keep a classical concept of God and meet the feminist critique. Naturally, we are not to think that the mere enunciation of a theology will help anything. The theology serves only as the theoretical background to the righting of injustices.

Absent from this inquiry are challenges to the validity of mystical experiences of God coming from arguments against the existence of God. If God does not exist, obviously no experiences could be really of God. I bracket these arguments here, as well as independent arguments for God's existence that would support the validity of mystical experiences of God. I do so for the sake of focusing on the issues most directly relevant to the topic at hand. For an ultimate appraisal of God-perceptions, therefore, the contents of this work will have to be related to the massive literature on arguments for and against the existence of God.

Notes

1   These include William Alston, 1991; Carolyn Franks Davis, 1989; Jerome Gellman, 1997 and 1998; Richard Swinburne, 1991 and 1996; William Wainwright, 1981; and Keith Yandell, 1993a and 1993b.

2   William Alston has defended the rationality of one's believing one has had a genuine mystical experience of God in Alston, 1991. Alston's approach, however, is different from the one taken by the above philosophers and myself. Alston argues for the rational justification of people participating in a socially recognized mystical 'doxastic practice' in which certain experiential input is taken as reason for believing God has appeared to them. Alston does not pretend to provide non-participants in a mystical practice with evidence of the validity of the practice. This differs from addressing the question of whether mystical experiences of God provide evidence that God is genuinely known by experience. If they do provide that evidence, they do so for mystics and for non-mystics alike. Even though Alston's approach differs from mine, I am greatly indebted to Alston for my understanding of the epistemological issues in discussing mystical experience.

3   These include Evan Fales, 1996a, 1996b and 2001; Richard Gale, 1994 and 1995; Michael Martin, 1990; and William Rowe, 1982.

4   We should not suppose that every person who has a mystical experience thinks or has the conceptual tools to realize that the experience is nonsensory or that the object is supersensory. That means that not all people who have a mystical experience need

know they have had one. It is no part of the meaning of 'mystical experience' that subjects know or believe they are having one, as defined here.

5 Seeing an extraordinary physical-like light, therefore, may be termed an 'anomalous' experience, but would not be a mystical experience in my characterization.

6 Classical Jewish mysticism, in particular, centers about Nothingness as the ultimate mystical object or state. See Matt, 1990.

7 Scientific studies of these and other anomalous experiences, including mystical ones, are summarized in Cardena et al., 2000.

8 In private communication, Richard Gale has suggested these kinds of events as constituting a non-mystical experience of God. I thank Gale for alerting me to the need to distinguish between 'experience' and 'mystical experience'.

9 Even if people would hear a voice, this voice would not literally be God's voice. So neither would there be a sensory perception (literally) of God.

10 Henceforth, for stylistic reasons I may sometimes omit the 'mystical' from the phrase, 'mystical experience of God'. Unless otherwise noted, therefore, from now on 'experience of God' is to mean, 'mystical experience of God'.

11 For a good example of a non-realist use of 'God', see D.Z. Phillips, 1981 and 1988.

12 This is the theme of Alston, 1991.

13 For a survey of mystical experiences of God in Islam see Schimmel, 1978; for Christianity see McGinn, 1991, and for Judaism see Jacobs, 1996.

Chapter 2

The Argument from Perception

In this chapter, I present the Argument from Perception in favor of God-perceptions (that is, mystical experiences of God) providing evidence that people have genuine experiential contact with God. I will be defending the view that the phenomenon of mystical experiences of God provides initial evidential sufficiency for the conclusion that human beings at least sometimes genuinely experience God. (From now on I will refer to this simply as the 'initial evidential sufficiency' of mystical experiences of God.) I dedicate the remaining chapters of this book to examining whether the initial evidence withstands reasons that could be advanced against there being genuine mystical experiences of God.

The Argument from Perception

The intuition behind the Argument from Perception is that since there are so many people who at various times in history have claimed to have theistic perceptions, there simply must be something to them. Of course there are deranged people, and others deceived about what they are undergoing, as well as people who are deceitful about what has happened to them. However, the phenomenon of alleged perceptual encounters with God is just too pervasive to think that it is all a mistake.

Philosophers who have defended the evidential value of God-perceptions have reasoned more or less in the manner of Richard Swinburne who enunciates this epistemic principle (1991, pp. 244–5): 'I suggest that it is a principle of rationality that (in the absence of special considerations) if it seems (epistemically) to a subject that x is present, then probably x is present.' What 'seems epistemically' to subjects is what they are inclined to believe based on the content of their present perceptual experience. Swinburne has argued that (1996, p. 138): '… the overwhelming testimony of so many millions of people to occasional experiences of God must, in the absence of counter-evidence of the kind analyzed, be taken as tipping the balance of evidence decisively in favour of the existence of God.' Swinburne adds the evidence of God-perceptions to other evidence to conclude that God exists. I, as well as others who have endorsed a Swinburne-like principle, have argued in the past that the testimony of experiences of God was sufficient by itself to justify the conclusion.[1] The idea is this. In ordinary sense perception, when a person seems to perceive something, unless we have positive

17

reason to doubt it, we take it that the person really perceived that thing. If a person attests to perceiving a table, we take it that a table presently exists and that the person sees it, if we see no special reason to doubt it. Perceptual claims can be discounted for one of two reasons: either because there is reason to doubt the alleged object is present when someone claims to perceive it, or because whether or not it is present there is reason to doubt the person is seeing it. The point is that we need a reason to doubt a sensory perceptual report in order not to accept it as true. Otherwise, we may take the sensory perceptual report, a report based on our perceptual experience, as sufficient evidence of its truth. Let's say, then, that ordinary sensory 'perceptual beliefs', beliefs formed on the basis of the content of sensory experience, enjoy 'initial evidential sufficiency'. This means that, in the absence of reasons against their validity, a person would be justified in taking such beliefs to be true.

Now mystical experience of God counts as perceptual no less than does sensory perception. Mystical experiences of God involve purportedly encountering God by means of experiencing a phenomenal content presenting its object to the subject. When people are appeared to through 'table-ish' phenomenal content, they think they perceive a table. In perceptions of God, when people are appeared to with 'God-ish' phenomenal content, they think they perceive God.

What grants sense-perception initial evidential sufficiency – and here is the central move in the Argument from Perception – is precisely its perceptual character. So, the argument goes, perceptual, mystical experience of God too should enjoy initial evidential sufficiency. Hence, if people *seem* to perceive God we should assume they really do perceive God, unless we come up with a reason to doubt it. Hence, perceptions of God enjoy initial evidential sufficiency.

The onus of proof, therefore, falls on the philosopher who wishes to deny the initial evidential sufficiency of perceptions of God. Such a person will have to advance good reasons for thinking that mystical experiences of God lack initial evidential sufficiency. So far, the argument concludes, no one has succeeded in advancing plausible reasons for discounting all or even most perceptions of God. Therefore, the initial situation prevails. There is sufficient evidence attesting to God's existing and appearing from time to time to human beings.

Matthew Bagger has objected to the 'protective intentions' of this sort of argument, for 'privileging one possible explanation', namely the theistic one (1999, p. 134). Referring to a version of it I put forth, he writes that the 'Oxford strategy appears even more baldly protective and illegitimate ... ' (1999, p. 134 – 'Oxford strategy' referring to the Swinburne-like style of reasoning). Bagger means to insist that the theistic explanation of God-perceptions not be favored over any alternative explanations.

However, the Argument from Perception does not pretend to unduly favor the theistic understanding of God-perceptions. True, the argument sets up the discussion in such a way that we start with a *prima facie* case for the genuineness of God-perceptions, and only then proceed to counter-arguments. However, that serves only as a way of ordering the discussion, and lacks intrinsic epistemological significance. At the end of the day the justification for thinking God-perceptions genuine will depend on the total relevant evidence, for and against, when weighed up all together. The order in which we place the evidence before us matters not at all. As long as the defender of the Argument from Perception is open to counter-arguments, therefore, no protective coating covers the manner of argumentation.

The point of putting the evidence of the Argument from Perception at the start has more to do with historical reasons than epistemological ones. Because before Swinburne prominent philosophers had little to say in favor of mystical experiences of God having any evidential value, and thought of them as mere 'subjective' states, it is good to start the discussion by declaring that such experiences do indeed carry at least initial evidential value.[2] Thereafter searching for possible counter-evidence no longer looks like a superfluous undertaking. The Argument from Perception, therefore, should be absolved of the charge of protective intentions.

Problems with the Argument from Perception

Nonetheless, while I have defended this argument in the past, I now believe this form of the Argument from Perception inadequately establishes the initial evidential sufficiency of God-perceptions. This is because the argument relies narrowly on a controversial epistemological approach. To adequately ground its conclusion we need to be able to cast the argument on a wider epistemological base. To elucidate this requirement, I turn to some critiques of the 'original' Argument from Perception.

John Zeis has rejected the Argument from Perception because he believes that the 'only evidence we have' for perceptual initial evidential sufficiency pertains to our perception of physical objects, implying we have no such evidence in the case of mystical experience of God (Zeis, 1999, p. 263). I am not sure what Zeis considers 'evidence' for initial evidential sufficiency. Perhaps he means that only for perceptual claims about physical objects do we have evidence that people *consider* their beliefs to have initial evidential sufficiency. Our usual way of acting on our sensory perceptions attests to this. If that were what Zeis meant, I would counter that we have similar evidence for beliefs based on theistic perceptions. People who have God-perceptions commonly make claims on that basis. Thus, our evidence for humans taking perception as a basis for true judgments includes the instance of perceptions of God. To be sure, instances of theistic perception are infrequent relative to the ubiquitous occurrence of sensory experiences. Nonetheless, the evidence that people who have perceptions of God take their experiences to be genuine need not be less important than the corresponding finding for sensory perception.[3]

Zeis may be objecting that sensory perceptions have initial evidential sufficiency only because of certain features peculiar to sensory perception not possessed by mystical perception. Therefore, we cannot conclude that mystical experiences have initial evidential sufficiency just because sensory perceptions do. I now turn to a detailed presentation of such a counter-argument, by Henry Levinson and Jonathan Malino, to the Argument from Perception.

Levinson and Malino have argued that a perception of any kind enjoys initial evidential sufficiency only when 'there are (a sufficient number of) intersubjective tests for the veridicality' of the perception, 'which have been performed and turned out positive, or which there is reason to believe would turn out positive if they were performed' (Levinson and Malino, 1999, p. 305).

They contend that there is not a 'sufficient number' of intersubjective tests in the case of perceptions of God that would 'turn out positive', as there is for sense perceptions. Therefore, perceptions of God lack initial evidential sufficiency.

Levinson and Malino, then, oppose seeing the evidential value of a perception resting solely on its perceptual character. In their view sensory perceptions are not evidential on their own solitary strength. Rather the network of intersubjective crosschecks appropriate to the context in which sensory perceptions occur confers their evidential status upon them. Lacking such a reliable intersubjective network, they claim, mystical perceptions fail to generate initial evidential sufficiency.

Here is the idea. When people seem to see a physical object, what makes the 'seeming' evidentially sufficient, that is, what justifies their concluding on evidence that they do see what they seem to see (if they base their belief on evidence at all), is not just that they seem to see the object. Rather, it is the present perceptual episode together with a rich network of background knowledge. The background knowledge includes what justifies them in assuming that if crosschecks were now to be performed these would turn out positive. If a person claims to see a tree, a number of tests are available to us to check on that claim. We can look in the same direction, can attempt to touch the tree, check if there are leaves on the ground nearby, check the person's eyesight, and so on.

Actual or potential agreement between tests creates the initial evidential status of the present tree-perception. We do not require that such tests actually be made. It's enough if we have reason to believe that were they to be made, they would give positive results. Ordinarily, such expectations exist in the example of someone claiming to see a tree. 'In [an] alleged tree experience', write Levinson and Malino (1999, p. 306):

> even if one does not run through any intersubjective tests of its veridicality, there
> is reason ... to believe such tests would turn out positive. The sheer ordinariness

of the alleged tree experience, and the mountain of evidence of the reliability of such reports based on experience, establishes a *strong presumption* in favor of any such report.

We have good reason to suppose that even when we do not perform checks on tree-perceptions, were we to perform them, they would give positive results. Hence, we deem a present tree-perception to confer evidence on there being a tree there, without having to perform any crosschecks. In the final analysis, though, the initial evidential sufficiency of tree-perceptions comes from the justified expectation that crosschecks would confirm the presence of a tree and that the person was seeing it.

The case is different for perceptions of God. Suppose a mystic claims to perceive God. The counter-argument points out that there is little anyone else, or even the mystic, could do that would confirm God was now present and genuinely perceived by that mystic. We may have reliable ways to check whether mystics *think* they perceive God, or whether it *seems* they are perceiving God. That is quite different, however, from possessing reliable checks that would confirm that God really was present and really was appearing to the subject. Hence, the crosscheck requirement stands unfulfilled for mystical experience of God. Hence, the Argument from Perception fails when it claims that mystical perception shares initial evidential sufficiency with sensory perception.

A related argument has been put forward by Evan Fales (2001), who argues that

> Crosschecking and crosscheckability must be integral parts of any perceptual epistemic practice because what a perceiver takes to be present on the basis of her experiences might not be what is in fact causally responsible for those experiences. Crosschecking 'pins down' stages of the causal process, thereby eliminating alternative hypotheses as to how the input is produced.

Fales goes on to make the point specifically for mystical experiences, listing three principles for vindicating crosschecking. Here are Fales' principles: inductive methods to determine causally relevant antecedent conditions; 'triangulating' the event by correlating it with other effects of the same purported cause; and (3) confirming causal mechanisms connecting a cause to its effects.

Alas, Fales claims, no successful system of crosschecking procedures exists or is likely to be forthcoming for mystical experiences of God. Therefore, the perceptual epistemic practice in which mystical experiences of God are embedded is severely defective.

These philosophers should not be taken to be contending we could never *imagine* adequate intersubjective crosschecks that would confirm mystical experiences of God. Rather they mean to argue, if I understand them correctly, that in fact we have no crosschecks of a sufficient degree of success for God-perceptions. Indeed, we can imagine highly successful crosschecks for mystical perceptions that would not fall so very far short of the success of crosschecks for sensory perception. Suppose, for example, all or almost all people reported mystical experiences of God much of the time. Suppose further that people regularly asked God, when in such an experience, whether God had appeared to so-and-so at that particular place and that particular time, as so-and-so had claimed. Suppose further that generally God replied in the affirmative. In that way a network of intersubjective crosschecks would have been built up, establishing the general reliability of God-perceptions to a very high degree. Of course the crosschecks would have to depend on the genuineness of perceptions of God for their validity, but the same applies to crosschecks for sensory perception. They too occur within sensory perception.

So we can easily imagine there being a rich fund of crosschecks that conferred a high degree of confirmation on mystical experiences of God. However, that will not help us answer the charge that there simply do not exist crosschecks of such honorable stature and that therefore we are not warranted in thinking mystical experiences of God possess even initial evidential value.

The Argument Reconstructed

I want to explain now why, nevertheless, mystical experiences of God do enjoy initial evidential sufficiency. This will require my revising the Argument from Perception. To motivate the form of the revision, I begin with an excursion into different approaches concerning the evidential link between perceptual episodes and the corresponding belief, the link between subjects seeming to see a tree and there being evidence for their belief that there is a tree they see. (I must warn that not all philosophers see the ordinary link between perception and belief in terms of evidence. Since, however, our topic is whether 'we' have *evidence* for God's being the actual object of mystical perception, we will focus on questions of evidence.) We will then return to apply the discussion to the dispute over the Argument from Perception.

Four Epistemologies

There are four leading epistemological theories as to how to go from sensory experience to justified beliefs about experience. They are 'foundationalism', 'coherentism', 'foundherentism' and 'conventionalism'.[4] The latter will be left aside for separate treatment in Chapter Four. At present, I use this terminology to present different views about how perceptual beliefs get evidentially justified.[5]

The first view is 'strong foundationalism'. Applied to sensory perception, the strong foundationalist maintains that a sensory belief (that is a belief formed on the basis of a sense perception) is sufficiently justified by the relevant sensory experience independent of any confirming beliefs or evidence.[6] Thus, your belief that there is a tree in front of you possesses evidential sufficiency solely due to its perceptually seeming to you that you see a tree. The evidence can be defeated by further considerations but, until it is, your belief has all the evidence it needs to be justified. The view is called 'foundationalist' because justification is ultimately *grounded* on sense-experience, and is 'strong' because of giving evidential sufficiency to the individual perception.

'Weak foundationalism', on the other hand, maintains that a sensory belief is justified somewhat, but not sufficiently, by the relevant sensory experience. That is, a sensory experience confers some degree of justification on the relevant sense belief, but not enough to constitute sufficient justification for that belief. When you perceptually seem to see a tree, you then have (only) some reason to think there is a tree that you are seeing, and that it is not a hallucination or a trick. However, the perceptual episode in itself does not provide sufficient evidence to warrant your belief that a tree stands before you. What else must you have for justification? The 'weak foundationalist', as I am using that term, requires support by other experiences. Your present impression that you see a tree gives you initial evidential sufficiency together with the rich background of perceptions of trees, and of other objects, by yourself and by others. Your present belief gains support by the accumulation of past experiences. The view remains 'foundationalist' because justification remains grounded on sense-experiences, but 'weak' because of the evidential inadequacy of an individual perception.

'Coherentism' says, roughly, that justification is wholly a matter of beliefs belonging together in a consistent, coherent set. 'Justification' results from mutual support among beliefs. In that case, no sensory belief gets evidential support of any kind from (what we consider) the 'relevant' sensory experience alone. From the start, your belief that you see a tree results from its integration into an entire system of consistent beliefs, the more coherent the better. Coherentism comes in various sophisticated versions. Here I will go along with the view that coherentism can succeed only if it grants a distinguished initial status to beliefs caused by sense perception. 'Modified coherentism', as I will call it, will still maintain that justification is wholly a matter of mutual support among beliefs, and that perceptual episodes *per se* do not provide justification, yet will allow that beliefs formed perceptually are such that cohering with them is especially good. In the end, though, when people find themselves with a belief that there is a tree before them, what justifies that belief is the way it integrates into all, or all relevant, beliefs they have.

Finally, 'foundherentism' as a midway position between foundationalism and coherentism, agrees with weak foundationalism that perceptual beliefs enjoy some initial evidential value apart from the context with which they cohere. Unlike weak foundationalism, though, foundherentism agrees with coherentism that sensory perceptual beliefs receive evidential support from the mutual support they enjoy together with other beliefs of a person. In turn, the initial evidential value of a sensory belief itself contributes to the evidential goodness of one's network of beliefs. Susan Haack, who coined the term 'foundherentism', compares the epistemological situation to that of a crossword puzzle (1993, Chapter Four). The puzzle presents clues and places for making entries. Clues give an initial, though inadequate, basis for an entry. Whether or not an entry is sufficiently grounded will depend, however, on how it meshes with the overall filling in of the puzzle. In the same way that the individual entry satisfies its clue, this helps support, in turn, the final pattern of entries. The clue gives the initial anchor to the entry, and contributes to overall confirmation, but ultimately the entry will enjoy evidential sufficiency only if it coheres well with the whole of the noetic structure of a person's beliefs. This also applies to a sensory belief and the whole of a person's belief structure.

Having briefly enumerated the leading theories on how perceptual beliefs get their initial evidential sufficiency, let us see now how the Argument from Perception and the counter-argument fit in to these views.

In effect, the Argument from Perception uses strong foundationalism when it argues that a sensory perceptual episode by itself provides initial evidential sufficiency to the relevant sensory belief. It can therefore proceed to argue the same for a mystical experience of God: it accords initial evidential sufficiency to the belief God has appeared until we come up with a reason to detract from this initial evidential.

Weak foundationalism, on the contrary, is congenial to the counter-argument against the Argument from Perception. Indeed, Levinson and Malino suggest a principle of epistemic justification to the effect that perceptual experience provides a 'small degree of evidential support', to be augmented by confirming intersubjective tests or by the justified assumption that such tests would be positive if performed (1999, p. 305). The intersubjective tests are meant to provide experiential confirmation to the original perceptual belief. Therefore, Malino and Levinson, and apparently Fales, have adopted a weak foundationalist epistemology.

Weak foundationalism challenges the Argument from Perception because in order to achieve initial evidential sufficiency a perception of God would have to enjoy a good degree of backing by evidence that further intersubjective tests would pan out were we to perform them. An isolated mystical episode will not be adequate. The counter-argument contends that the backing is not forthcoming so that perceptions of God do not enjoy initial evidential sufficiency, the Argument from Perception notwithstanding.

Modified coherentism and foundherentism also challenge the Argument from Perception. According to the former, we would have to look beyond an isolated perceptual belief about God before we could know whether it had any evidential worth, let alone sufficient evidential worth. Our look beyond would have to consider the mutual support of a vast number of beliefs, which are justified together, and include the perceptual belief about God. A counter-argument based on this approach would contend that mystical claims about God do not cohere well with our overall network of beliefs. Foundherentism, too, would require going beyond the 'clue' of the perceptually formed belief about God to see how well that belief coheres with much else that we believe in a mutual-supporting complex of beliefs. A counter-argument from this direction would argue that the initial evidential worth of a mystical episode is neutralized or overruled by the failure of the relevant belief to mesh with the surrounding belief structure.

It is not my place to try to defend strong foundationalism, and thus the original Argument from Perception, against the other epistemological theories. Philosophers greater and better than I will have to help us there. My interest here is whether a plausible 'Argument from Perception' can be formulated given any one of the other epistemologies.

With weak foundationalism, a plausible Argument from Perception must come up with crosschecks confirming a present perception of God or with reason to think crosschecks if performed would be successful. This would provide reason to think that perceptions of God were evidentially acceptable at least until proven otherwise. With modified coherentism, a plausible argument would have to show that it at least appears to be the case that perceptual beliefs about God participate in a highly coherent set of mutually supporting beliefs. For foundherentism, a plausible argument would show that it at least appears to be the case that the surrounding complex of beliefs strengthens the initial evidential value of a mystical perception of God.

Since weak foundationalism drives the counter-arguments of Malino and Levinson, and Fales, respectively, in what follows I will formulate my reply in those terms. Although coherentists and foundherentists will differ with foundationalists over the nature of the permissible 'evidence', the discussion that follows, restricted to weak foundationalism, is relevant to the former positions as well. If I can show, as I hope to, that adequate crosschecks exist for mystical experiences of God, then that will be relevant for how these views, too, assess the final evidential situation, when all the facts are in. I leave it to the reader who favors one of the other epistemologies to make the necessary adjustments in my argument for their epistemology for themselves.

A Weak-foundationalist Version of the Argument from Perception

I want to show now that a plausible Argument from Perception can be given in weak foundationalist terms. To do so we must attend first to a few important distinctions. The first is the distinction between a particular person being justified in believing that person's present mystical perception of God to be veridical, and 'our' believing there are veridical mystical experiences of God. These are not the same issues. It could turn out that on no specific occasion has a person ever been perceptually warranted in believing God had appeared. Yet when we looked at the available evidence over history we might be justified in believing that at least some perceptions of God are veridical. Compare the situation to one in which no witness at a murder trial saw enough of what transpired on the night of the murder to be justified in concluding that Jones was the murderer. Yet members of the jury who hear the testimony of all the witnesses may very well have more than enough evidence to conclude that Jones was the murderer. The jurors possess more evidence than any single witness, and we possess more evidence about the history of perceptions of God than most persons who have thought they were in real contact with God.

The counter-argument against the Argument from Perception, as we have seen, proceeds by casting doubt on whether an individual mystical episode carries justification for thinking it was genuinely of God. I suggest this issue carries less vital philosophical significance than the question of whether *we* are justified in thinking that there have been cases of real contact with God by mystical perception.

A second distinction I want to make is that between the requirement that there be confirming evidence (or the expectation that there will be if we looked for it) for an individual perceptual episode, and the quite different requirement that the confirming evidence be of the kind forthcoming for sensory perception. The former requirement plausibly applies to mystical perceptions, given weak foundationalist assumptions. The latter does not. 'Confirming evidence' for a belief based on a God-perception need not be of the type (or of the degree) we enjoy for perceptions of physical objects.

We should not tie our notion of confirming evidence to that associated with sensory perception, as involving the sorts of 'tests' available there. For example, having others just 'take a look' constitutes a good crosscheck for many sensory claims, say about the presence of a tree. It would be a mistake, though, to build-in on conceptual grounds having others just 'take a look' as a crosschecking requirement for all types of perceptual claims, including the mystical (and including many sensory ones as well, by the way). The requirement here should be 'confirming empirical evidence', *be it what it may*. If God sightings do not have much confirming empirical evidence, *be it what it may*, they will remain unjustified for that reason, and not because they lack crosschecks appropriate to sensory claims about physical objects.

Perhaps a counter-arguer will reply that, while I might be right on the conceptual issue, we still have good reason to require sensory-type crosschecks in the case of perceptions of God. That is because justification of physical object claims based on sensory perception should be our 'evidential standard'. That's because only where crosschecks of the physical-object kind are available do we get in fact sufficient justification for a perceptual contention. Anything less falls short of evidential sufficiency. This contention is not a conceptual claim about 'confirming evidence' or 'evidential sufficiency', but a statement about what we are to expect based on experience on the ground. We know by experience that without crosschecks of the kind appropriate to physical-object claims we just do not get justification. So we are within our rights to insist that mystical claims pass tests that physical-object claims pass.

The counter-arguer's contention is wholly gratuitous, I fear. There is no good reason to make physical-object claims our evidential standard. Why should we? Our ordinary physical-object beliefs are way overjustified by confirming evidence. We have extremely luxurious constellations of confirming networks there. Hence it does not follow that were mystical claims justified to a lesser degree than that, or not by similar procedures, that they would be *un*justified. All that would follow would be that they enjoyed less justification than belief in physical object statements, but perhaps be justified nonetheless.

The requirement that all types of perception, including the mystical type, be judged by sensory-type tests does not represent so much a plausible epistemological view as it reflects our being spoiled by the deluxe evidence we have for our sensory perceptual claims. Being used to a certain very high degree of confirmation in the case of sensory claims about physical objects, counter-arguers have decided to insist on the same elsewhere. I suggest we judge the extent of confirming evidence for individual perceptions of God on its own terms, by what is appropriate to it, and not by comparing it to sensory claims.

The unwarranted insistence that mystical experiences of God abide by the same standards of confirmation as sensory experience might be driven by what I would call the 'next-thing-you-know' syndrome. The 'NTYK' syndrome manifests when people resist a philosophical argument not on its own demerits, but because were they to accept it they would then have to face what they expect to be the next stage in the argument, which they reject in advance. The NTYK syndrome sometimes affects discussions about God's existence. If someone were to accept an argument showing that God exists, this in itself would require no religious conversion or thinking that any theistic religions were true, or even near the truth. God might exist even if all theistic religions were wanting. Yet, people might resist an argument for God's existence because feeling that 'the-next-thing-you-know' they will be facing attempts to convince them of the truth of Judaism, Christianity or Islam, which they reject out of hand. The potential for the NTYK syndrome exists when the topic is God because typically philosophers identified as religious adherents are the ones backing arguments for God's existence. So, the fear of being maneuvered into someone's favorite place of worship hangs over the discussion like a dark cloud threatening a downpour.

Returning to our topic, the NTYK syndrome may motivate an insistence on an unjustified standard of evidence, in the following way. Some people might imagine themselves never assenting to any religion, no matter how liberal, unless the evidence for it were very high, as high, say, as the evidence for the world of physical objects. After all, religions wish to be quite demanding of one's behavior, emotions and intellectual energies. These people might think the cost of religion too high to buy into it without a commensurate grounding. Driven by the NTYK fear, they might try to jack-up the requirements for an argument for God's really being experienced and thus existing to the level of those they would insist on in the expected, or dreaded, next move by their opponents.

I suggest that the question whether people know God in experience, and thus that God exists, be treated as a philosophical issue worthy of debate independent of the question of whether any theistic religion is rationally acceptable. The question bears intrinsic interest and has implications for people's lives short of religious conversion. I suggest therefore that the NTYK syndrome be neutralized. It might turn out that even if we were to conclude that people genuinely perceived God, and that God existed, the strength of that conclusion would fall short of what some would require to take religion seriously.

I have now distinguished between the question whether a particular mystic is justified in thinking a specific perception of God is veridical, and whether we, looking at the phenomenon of theistic mysticism, are justified in believing that there is validity to the phenomenon of theistic mysticism. And I have distinguished between the requirement that there be just 'sufficient confirm-ing evidence' for theistic perceptions, be it what it may, and the demand that the confirming evidence be of the sort and of the power we get for sensory perceptual claims. My conclusion is that we should be looking at whether we are justified in taking perceptions of God as veridical, and that we do so simply in terms of confirming evidence, be it what it may, and not insist on a degree of confirmation similar to what we obtain for sensory perception. On those terms, I turn to consider the initial evidential case for the veracity of mystical experiences of God from a weak foundationalist approach.

Numbers, diversity and vividness   For my first witness I call upon features of God-perceptions: their numbers, diversity and sometime vividness. Each perception carries positive evidential value toward its own validity, falling short of initial evidential sufficiency, on weak foundationalist assumptions. Each such episode, nonetheless, receives support from the numerous such experiences that have been reported over time across various religions and cultures. These reports occur in 'professional' mystical literature as well as at the level of 'everyday' mystical perceptions. Western religions include traditions reflecting mystical perceptions of God, and Indian religions too include mystical reports that should be deemed equivalent to perceptions of God.[7] In addition, the scholarly literature supplies reports of ordinary peo-ple who have experienced what they took to be direct perceptions of God being present to them.[8]

The sheer incidence of such mystical episodes over time, across religions and cultures constitutes confirming evidence in favor of any given perception of God being veridical. Furthermore, studies have documented the prevalence of 'ordinary' people having experiences of a 'mysterious' presence or of a 'higher power'. These too count toward confirming the validity of theistic perceptions, especially on the generic concept of God. Although these are not reported to be perceptions of God, nonetheless that such experiences occur strengthens the evidential force of the many reported explicit God-sightings. If God-sightings are veridical, we should expect there might be incomplete or partial experiences of God in addition to full-blown ones. Experiences of just a 'higher power' increase the chances that God exists, then, the same as noticing just that someone or other is in the room (rather than no one) raises the chances that Jones is in the room. When looking for confirming evidence, then, a 'sense of presence' and a perception of just a 'higher power' cohere well with mystical experiences of God and add to the confirming evidence.

Reports of a mysterious presence or perception of a higher power may, I admit, receive explanation in terms of realities other than God. I contend only that when considered in light of the history of perceptions of God they provide further confirming evidence. Deriders would do well to be reminded here of William Alston's argument that evidence can count in favor of a given hypothesis even if it also counts in favor of some competing hypothesis. Consider, for example the three hypotheses: (1) No one is in the room, (2) Exactly two people are in the room, and (3) Exactly three people are in the room. Suppose you give a quick look at only one corner of the room and see someone there. Your observation counts against (1) and at the same time increases the chances in favor of both (2) and (3), although the latter two are logically inconsistent (Alston, 1993).

It is not only the sheer number of God-perceptions that count in favor of their theistic interpretation. There is a further confirming factor. Often, subjects report on the vividness of their experiences and the consequent certainty of God's reality as revealed in their experiences. Vividness of God-perceptions helps convince some of those mystics that God's existence is better grounded than objects of their ordinary perception. Everything else being equal, the more vivid and convincing a perception, the greater should be its contribution to the evidential case for the existence of its object. Hence, the vividness of many God-perceptions adds to the case for their validity. No doubt, some will have other ideas for accounting for the vividness and certainty accompanying mystical experiences of God. At this point, though, I am interested in making only an initial, not a conclusive, evidential case, before considering undermining evidence.

Recognizing the evidential force of the impressive array of perceptions of God need not blind us to the need to invalidate many God-sightings. No doubt the history of mystical reports of experiencing God, as well as reports of a sense of a higher presence, include many experiences we should dismiss as pathological, staged, or unduly influenced by social pressures and expectations. I do not recommend naivety. At this stage of the discussion,

however, I am building a case only for initial evidential sufficiency, in weak
foundationalist terms, for the over-all validity of the phenomenon of perceptions of God. My contention is that the numbers and varied circumstances of
perceptions of God should be included among evidence tending to confirm
the validity of the perceptions. Later, of course, it will be time to consider
disconfirming evidence to be marshaled against the confirming evidence. It
remains to be seen, for instance, whether enough episodes of God perceptions can be 'explained away' or nullified to sufficiently weaken the confirming force of the phenomenon of mystical experiences of God. Below I
summarize an earlier discussion of mine of a cluster of alternative treatments of mystical experiences of God that fail to nullify enough mystical
episodes to make a dent in the evidence, and in Chapters Four and Five I
will be considering further proposed alternative explanations. Meanwhile,
I continue to list confirming evidence for an opening case for the validity
of perceptions of God.

A checking procedure   Despite the claims of the counter-arguers, a kind of
intersubjective checking presents itself for perceptions of God. There is
such a thing as trying to 'take a look', to check whether perceptions of God
are veridical, since mystical traditions provide procedures for aspiring to a
mystical perception of God. The common denominator of these spiritual
regimens is the achievement of self-nullification, in the sense of annulling
(as much as possible) one's egocentric way of being in the world. Mystical
traditions have been most impressed by loss of egocentrism as a way of
getting into position for perceiving God. Plausibly, an ability to perceive
outside of an egocentric framework of reference aids recognition of a reality
such as God, who will be recognized as possessed of (in some sense)
supreme value.[9]

Undeniably, reports of mystical experiences of God do occur outside
mystical traditions, to ordinary folk, sometimes quite unexpectedly and with
no prior preparation. Although many such people may perhaps have reached
a degree of non-egocentrism, a regimen of self-nullification does not count
as a necessary condition of having mystical experiences of God. Even so,
procedures do exist for achieving mystical illumination which, if successful,
would count in favor of one's having had a veridical experience of God.
Here, then, is one way of 'checking' on whether others have had perceptions
of God: follow a regimen of self-nullification and see what happens.[10] Of
course, all might be victims of delusion, thinking they had experiential
contact with God when they really did not. At this point of the discussion,
however, this point is not relevant. A similar point could be made about
crosschecking of physical object claims. Perhaps they are all delusory, or if
that surpasses credulity, perhaps many more are delusory than we think. On
weak foundationalist principles, however, that a perception is delusory has
to be shown, given the initial case of crosscheck confirmation. The same
applies to claims about perceiving God. If there are crosscheck successes or

expectation of success, then that the experiences are all delusory has to be shown, given the initial favorable findings.

Of course, the mystical checking procedures lack the facility and immediacy of just looking to see whether a table is in the room. Mystical training may extend over long periods, and no one can determine the time at which mystical perceptions are 'supposed' to arrive. Also, the taking of a look is not tied to the close geographical vicinity. That is, being at the same place as a person who experiences God when trying to also experience God has no significance. This is because geographical vicinity is relevant to stable physical objects. Since God is not a physical object, geographical vicinity plays no role.

Neither does simultaneity play a role in checking perceptions of God. That is, there is no significance to being able to have a confirming perception of God at the same time that someone else perceives God. This for two reasons. The first is that the person who is 'checking' may not have embarked on an egocentric nullifying path in time, so may not be in a position to test a claim to a current experience of God. Secondly, God cannot be expected to appear as automatically as a table, when you look for it. God has been experienced as a self-initiating reality, in some sense, rather than as inert, so that whether a person perceives God will be, in part, up to God, as it were. So even a person who has surpassed egocentric concerns should not be expected to experience God all the time or whenever choosing. In particular, God can appear to one person and not to another.

In some respects (though not in all), mystical training as 'checking' resembles training for checking whether the Mexican spotted owl lives in a designated area of New Mexico. Training as a bird-watcher provides a way of putting yourself in position to find a Mexican spotted owl if it is there. Otherwise, you would likely not know how to look for the bird in the first place, might not discern the bird from the background, and might not be able to determine the markings of a bird you saw. Bird-watcher training, though, is not a necessary condition for sighting Mexican spotted owls. A novice might succeed in the task. Neither is it a sufficient condition. No one can determine just when a sought after bird will appear in one's binoculars. Mexican spotted owls have minds of their own and do not fit neatly into planned tests. Bird-watching training will fail to guarantee success even if the Mexican spotted owl is there to be found. Also, one person may detect the owl's presence while a second person fails to do so (even at the same observation point). Finally, failing to see a bird after close, extended watching may count for something against the hypothesis that the bird lives in the area, but positive sightings count far more in favor. That's because an observer might fail to see a bird only because the bird is hiding or simply not in that part of the zone being investigated. If a Mexican spotted owl is sighted, however, that counts more in the positive direction than does a failure to sight.

Therefore I add a second consideration counting in favor of the validity of God sightings. A significant number of God-sightings issue from a (lengthy) training for getting oneself into position to be able to perceive God. Nothing guarantees that God will appear at the end of the process, yet the fact that specified steps do sometimes issue in experiences of God's presence, give us a checking procedure the (sometime) success of which counts further in favor of the validity of perceptions of God.

The effects of mystical episodes   Yet a third witness contributes to confirming the validity of mystical experiences of God: the effects of mystical episodes. William Wainwright has suggested several 'independent tests' of this type for distinguishing experiences of God that are veridical from those that are not (Wainwright, 1981, pp. 86–8). Three of Wainwright's tests are relevant to making my case for the initial evidential sufficiency of perceptions of God.

Firstly, Wainwright writes that the 'consequences of the experience must be good for the mystic' (p. 86). If a perception of God does have such an effect, those consequences count in favor of the authenticity of the perception. This follows because we should expect that an experience of God would result in fruitful moral and spiritual signs. A person's coming out of God-experiences propelled toward an evil, egocentric life, would count strongly against the authenticity of the experience. If a person were to seem morally and spiritually unaffected, that too would count against the veracity of the mystical perceptions of that person.

One might want to advance support for some opposing explanation for the moral and spiritual betterment of subjects who have had perceptions of God. However, at this point I am saying only that Wainwright's criterion *counts toward* the initial evidential sufficiency of perceptions of God. This status is achieved when we have enough to go on to justify relying on a perception of God, before turning to negative considerations.

Now, the history of God-mysticism is replete with people, professional mystics and others, who, at least as far as we can tell, display saintliness and holiness, augmented and deepened by their experiences. So, here we have additional initial evidence in favor of validity. To be sure that history also includes subjects apparently bent on evil and destruction subsequent to mystical experiences of God. We should take their immoral stature to count against the authenticity of their experiences.

A second test advanced by Wainwright is that a person's perceptions of God should prove 'fruitful and edifying' for others. We can test a God-perception, then, by checking the influence of the subject on society. This too follows from what we should expect from an experience supposed to be of a reality like God. Discounting negative instances, we apparently have plenty of instances of the positive social influence of persons graced with mystical God-perceptions.

Thirdly, Wainwright offers the 'profundity, and the 'sweetness' of what the mystic has to say as counting in favor of the authenticity of the mystic's experience (p. 87). The insignificance or inanity of what the mystic says counts against authenticity. When God is the alleged object, we should expect an experience not to result in silliness or trifling matters. Here too, we have plenty of evidence favoring this test of authenticity.

I conclude that these three tests suggested by Wainwright strengthen a weak-foundationalist case for the validity of perceptions of God.

Neuropsychological research   Finally, for a fourth source of confirming evidence I call to the stand neuropsychological research. Research is increasingly supporting the conclusion that unique processes in the brain accompany experiences of God. Researchers are divided over the correct theory. Noting unusual activity of the right hemisphere of the brain, some researchers opt for that as the physiological locus for mystical brain activity (Fenwick, 1996, and Batson, Schoenrade and Ventis, 1993). Research on epilepsy has led others to pin their hopes for understanding at least some mystical experiences on activity in the temporal lobes of the brain (see Bear and Fedio, 1977; Geschwind, 1983; Persinger, 1984, 1987, and 1983). And there are theories solely for meditative mystical experiences (Austin, 1998). A more comprehensive theory, claiming to cover a variety of mystical experiences as well as both meditative and non-meditative experiences, that has attracted attention is that of Eugene d'Aquili and Andrew Newberg (see d'Aquili and Newberg, 1993, 1999 and 2000). Increasingly, then, brain physiologists are convinced that mystical experiences are generated by unique brain activity.

I will be discussing some neuropsychological theories in some detail in Chapter 5. Here I wish to indicate that, everything else being equal, if unique brain activity is involved in mystical experiences, that counts in favor of the validity of those experiences. To see this, imagine that brain physiologists, after searching high and low, concluded that no unique brain activity occurred with mystical episodes. It seems clear that we would think this tended to disconfirm the validity of such experiences and would tend toward assimilating them with other experiences, including hyper-suggestive episodes, pathological disturbances and self-deceptive impressions. Assimilation with other experiences would explain why no unique brain activity occurred in mystical episodes. Therefore, that brain physiologists are beginning to discover unique brain activities or formations associated with mystical episodes must count in favor of their validity.

Compare the situation to an imaginary one in which an impressive number of people were to report hearing sounds humans generally did not hear. One way of investigating the validity of their claims would surely be to try to determine whether these people possessed relevant unusual brain formations or displayed appropriate extraordinary brain processes at the time they claimed to hear the unusual sounds. If they did, then, everything else being equal, this would tend to support, though not prove, that these people were having unusual experiences. Just so, the discovery of special brain activity connected with mystical experiences of God would, everything else being equal, tend to confirm the validity of reports of God-perceptions.

The sounds example differs from the mystical case in that we already have experience with sounds in any case, and we have reason to believe certain animals hear sounds humans do not hear. So in the sounds case we have confirming evidence around the claims that a person hears sounds other humans miss. So the sounds example should be more convincing than our mystical case. Nonetheless, it cannot be denied that, everything else being equal, the discovery of appropriate brain activity would help support the Argument from Perception.

Now, strictly speaking, the neuropsychological consideration counts in favor of the validity of mystical experiences other than those of God, as well. Yet, any evidence that counts in favor of the veracity of mystical experiences in general will thereby also count in favor of mystical experiences of God in particular. This means that some mystical claims that compete with theistic ones might also receive evidential support from brain research. Nonetheless, brain research does add to the case for the validity of God-perceptions.

I am well aware that from neuropsychological findings some readers will want to reach an opposite conclusion from the one I am presently urging. Namely, they will point to such findings as tending to confirm that mystical experiences of God are 'all in the head'. Later, I will argue that this way of thinking would be in error, and that we should not expect neurophysiological findings to confirm the illusory nature of God-perceptions.

I submit that the four considerations I have listed create initial evidential sufficiency for the validity, in enough cases, of the phenomenon of perception of God. In order to support this contention, I will now consider three possible sources of resistance to this conclusion.

Resistance to the Argument

Someone might resist acknowledging that the phenomenon of mystical experience of God has initial evidential sufficiency because of the negative evidence they think they have against its validity. So reasoning would be a mistake, however. To say that something has 'initial' evidential sufficiency means only that one has good reason to accept its validity until finding sufficient evidence against its validity. To appreciate the initial evidential sufficiency of perceptions of God, consider what we would naturally conclude from the evidence I have presented, were we to come up empty handed in a search for counter-evidence. It is clear that, if we did not allow our beliefs about sufficient counter-evidence to enter our judgment, the phenomenon of perceptions of God would enjoy initial evidential sufficiency.

A second reason for resistance to my conclusion might be that the evidence does not begin to approach the richness of crosschecking available for claims about physical objects. However, I have already argued the unacceptability of holding perceptions of God to the same types and standards of evidence as for perceptions of physical objects. So this source of resistance to my assessment should be resisted.

Finally, one may feel that the evidence, even in the absence of sufficient counter-evidence, hardly warrants the kind of faith-commitment required of religions that recognize valid perceptions of God. The evidence is just too poor to justify people's devoting themselves to a religious life. The phenomenon of perception of God does not enjoy initial evidential sufficiency for that!

My reply consists in reminding once again that the objector is misunderstanding the enterprise of examining the evidence provided by perceptions of God. Perhaps because philosophers who defend the validity of the phenomenon are often known to hold religious beliefs, others perceive the enterprise from the start as an opening move in an extended argument for some religious belief or other. However, the question of the validity of perceptions of God should stand on its own as a topic for philosophical inquiry, independent of its ramifications for joining in to a religious faith. Perhaps there is sufficient evidence for the existence of God, as experienced in theistic mystical experience, yet not enough evidence in favor of an entire religious system of belief. As long as such a possibility exists, the third source of resistance is a form of the 'the-next-thing–you-know' syndrome, and ought to be rejected.

I conclude that the Argument from Perception for the initial evidential sufficiency of mystical experiences of God is vindicated when recast as a weak-foundationalist argument.

A Cluster of Objections

For the Argument from Perception to succeed it must survive objections that would validly counter its evidence. The remainder of this book is dedicated to a detailed consideration of three important types of objections to the Argument from Perception. I close this chapter with a brief summary of my treatment of three objections to the Argument from Perception that I do not deal with here because I have done so in my previous book (Gellman, 1997). I ask the reader to refer to that work for the details of my argument.

Objection One

A great number of people are never graced with mystical experiences of God. In fact, quite clearly more people fail to experience God than do so. The absence of such experiences on the part of so many people counts impressively against the theistic explanation. This more than counterbalances the known mystical experiences.

Objection Two

There is no way to discover empirically that a mystical experience of God was delusory, that is that people were not in contact with God when they thought they were. However, if there is no possible way to show that an experience is delusory, the experience cannot possibly be positive evidence for its genuineness. Hence mystical experiences of God cannot count toward their own genuineness.

Objection Three

The diversity of religious experiences across religions and cultures prohibits taking any one type of experience as valid more than any other type. Why take God-experiences as valid and not experiences of Zeus? Furthermore, is the God discovered in experience supposed to be a Jewish God? A Christian or Muslim God? Since religions give such conflicting accounts of what God is like, wisdom would dictate we accept no mystical experiences of God as valid. Finally, why prefer mystical experiences of a personal God to those of an impersonal absolute being, when the latter too occur in impressive numbers and diversity of conditions?

Responses to the Objections

My response to the first objection was that since God was presumed to be a self-initiating being, and so had a say in who would experience God, we could not assume that failure to experience God was due to God's not being there to be perceived. Therefore, we could not equate the absence of a perception of God with experiencing God's absence. In addition, as mentioned above, judging from reports of God-sightings it would appear that training in non-egocentrism or 'decentering' of the self was important for having mystical experiences of God. Hence, whether the conditions for experiencing God obtained when someone failed to experience God, would be hard to determine (Gellman, 1997, Chapter Three).

My response to the second objection stated first that the ways of showing God-perceptions to be delusory would surely differ from sensory perception. Indeed, there were ways peculiar to its type of perception to show theistic mystical experiences to be probably delusory. For example, if a person were selfish and abusive to others before and continuing well after claiming to have perceived God, that would be a reason, everything else being equal, for thinking the perception probably delusory. We would have a positive reason for thinking the episode delusory.

I argued further that the possibility of finding reasons for thinking a perception was delusory was not a condition for a perception counting as evidence for its validity. It was sufficient that the perception be exposed to our discovering that even if the perception were not genuine it would have occurred anyway. That possibility and its not materializing would be a good reason for taking a perception as evidentially worthwhile. God-perceptions are exposed to such a test, in the form of the possibility of alternative naturalistic explanations. Alternative explanations propose that subjects have had God-perceptions under certain naturalistic conditions and that subjects would have had those perceptions even had they been not genuine. In this way the evidential value of a God-perception could be exposed to defeat (that is, would lose its evidential value), even if we had no idea how to find reasons for thinking it delusory (that is, showing it to be an inauthentic experience).

In my response to the third objection, from diversity, I argued firstly, among other responses, that mystical experiences of gods were evidentially far poorer than the corresponding experiences of God. This for two reasons. The first is that the former lack the impressive variety, cultural, historical and individual, of conditions under which God-perceptions occur. The second reason is that typically perceptual reports of gods are intertwined with bizarre and fantastic elements that greatly detract from their evidential worth.

Secondly, I argued that diversity between mystical experiences of God across religions and between a personal and a non-personal absolute was not a reason to abandon the evidence for genuine experiences of God. Generally, when faced with massive conflicting data, wisdom dictates that we seek a hypothesis that will best explain all of the data rather than discard our data entirely. For that reason I proposed seeking an overarching interpretation of mystical experience that would save as much of the diverse data as possible. For this purpose I proposed taking seriously the theme found in various mystical traditions of the sense of a hidden infinite plenitude of the reality known in mystical experience. The particular features revealed in mystical experiences are then perceived as being revealed out of that hidden plenitude. Using this idea we would reconcile diverse mystical perceptions as expressions of different features belonging to the one revealed reality. I offered this as one possibility for reconciliation, insisting only that the diversity of such a large collection of data, of mystical experiences, could not be a reason for abandoning the data altogether. My proposal should be distinguished from John Hick's 'pluralist hypothesis' that implies that none of the phenomenal features of an object of mystical experience belong to it (see Hick, 1989).

This completes my presentation of the revised Argument from Perception and my brief review of three objections to it.

Notes

1   See Gellman, 1997. Also Davis, 1989, and Keith Yandell, 1993a and 1999, have advanced an argument of this sort.

2   A classic example of the 'purely subjective' approach is C.B. Martin, 1955.
3   Perhaps Zeis means to require universal or near-universal agreement on the evidential value of a type of perception. If so he would be correct to point out a severe lack of such for God-perceptions. However, it is not clear this would show a lack of initial evidential sufficiency for God-perceptions. The absence of agreement here might be attributed to people having reasons against the validity of God-perceptions, resulting in an ultimate denial of evidential sufficiency. In that case, lack of agreement on (ultimate) evidential worth would be consistent with agreement on *initial* evidential value.
4   A fifth view is 'virtue epistemology', but pertains less directly to our present topic than the others, so I omit it from the present discussion (see Zagzebski, 1996). Other epistemological theories, such as reliabilism, do not deal with issues of evidential justification.
5   My presentation of the various epistemological views is indebted to Haack, 1993, Chapter One.
6   John Pollock, 1974, took this position at one time (see Chapter Two).
7   For an example, see M., *The Gospel of Ramakrishna*, 1964, containing a record of a devotee's association with Sri Ramakrishna.
8   See Hardy, 1980; James, 1958; Beardsworth, 1977; and Unger, 1976.
9   Some feminist thinkers have condemned the requirement of non-egocentrism as reflecting a male bias. The idea is that self-assertion and a will-to-power are typical male sins, requiring severe restriction for the life of the spirit. Women's sin has been quite the opposite, a lack of self-assertiveness and a readiness to offer oneself to subjugation by others. Thus women have to overcome a weak or underdeveloped ego, not labor to deflate their egos. An emphasis on non-egocentric attitudes thus damages the well-being of women and supports their oppression in society. For this critique, see for example, Goldstein Saiving, 1992, and Hampson, 1990. So it is important to point out that what I have in mind by a non-egocentric stance in the world should not entail a willingness to be unjustly subjugated by other human beings nor does it involve a denial of self-assertiveness when that is appropriate in human relations. For a good idea of how such non-egocentrism would look, I recommend Coakley, 1996.
10 Here we come up against the obvious fact that in various religious traditions the mentioned regimen issues in decidedly non-theistic experiences. This is the problem of diversity of mystical experiences that I have dealt with elsewhere (Gellman, 1997, Chapter Four).

Chapter 3

God's Non-dimensionality and Mystical Experience of God

In the previous chapter, I presented an Argument from Perception to the effect that the phenomenon of perceptions of God enjoys initial evidential sufficiency. The argument depended especially on noting the large number of God-perceptions in history, occurring across a rich variety of conditions. In this chapter, I examine an astute objection of Richard Gale's that threatens to undermine the evidential force of perceptions of God (Gale 1994 and 1995).

I will be discussing two versions of Gale's argument, the 'conceptual argument', and the 'epistemological argument'. Both arguments proceed from God's lack of dimensionality, 'dimensionality' denoting existence in both space and time. Even if on some theologies God exists within time, on no theology does God exist in space. So God lacks dimensionality. On Gale's conceptual argument, in principle it is impossible for a person to have a veridical perception of God, because there is a conceptual incoherence in the very idea of it. God could not possibly be a 'perceptual particular', that is: a substantive, enduring being appearing perceptually to a person. For an object to be a perceptual particular, it is enough that in principle it could appear to someone, whether or not anyone knew that it was appearing. The denial of perceptual particularity is, then, a conceptual and not an epistemological objection to the possibility of mystical experiences of God.

The epistemological argument, in contrast, claims that whether or not we can veridically perceive God, in the sense of God really being an object of our perception, we could never have good reason to think we had perceived God. God is forever beyond our perceptual knowledge. If either of these arguments were to succeed, the Argument from Perception would collapse.

Gale's Conceptual Argument

I begin with the conceptual argument for the conclusion that there is a conceptual incoherence in supposing God to be a perceptual particular.

According to Gale, in order for us to have a coherent concept of a particular object as a perceptual particular, a number of conditions must be met. These are as follows:

1   We must be able to understand what it means for the object to exist
    when not perceived. If the object is to be a substantive being, and not an
    illusory appearance only, we must understand what it means for it to
    exist when nobody perceives it.
2   The object must be able to be the common object of different percep-
    tions. It must make sense to think of various people perceiving the
    object (at one time or at different times) or for one person to perceive
    the object on various occasions.
3   We must be able to understand the distinction between numerical and
    qualitative identity with regard to the object. That is, we must be able to
    give meaning to the distinction between that very object being perceived
    on different occasions, on the one hand, and other objects qualitatively
    identical to it (that 'look' like it), but numerically distinct from it, being
    perceived instead. After all, there could be two distinct, perceptually
    indistinguishable objects. We must possess a conceptual apparatus for
    making the distinction between the same object recurring in perception,
    and two perceptually indistinguishable objects appearing in distinct per-
    ceptual episodes.

   We need these requirements, maintains Gale, to distinguish between perceptual particulars and mere 'phenomenal particulars', particulars private to
one's perception. The chair in my room is a perceptual particular, while my
chair-like visual image of the chair is a phenomenal particular, the latter
existing only as long as it remains with me. A phenomenal particular exists
only when perceived. A perceptual particular does not. A phenomenal particular cannot be a common object of different perceptions, whether of one
subject or several subjects. If you have a chair-like visual image and I have
one, no matter how qualitatively similar they may be they are two distinct
phenomenal particulars. A perceptual particular, on the other hand, can be a
common object of different perceptions. Finally, since each occurrence of a
phenomenal particular presents a phenomenal particular numerically distinct from one presented in any other occurrence, there is no application to
phenomenal particulars of the distinction between qualitative and numerical
identity across experiences. No phenomenal particulars are numerically identical across experiences.
   Physical objects are perceptual particulars, contends Gale, thanks to their
spatial-temporal locations. These locations make possible the very idea of a
physical object existing when we do not perceive it, since it can be thought
of as existing at time and place coordinates when and where nobody perceives it. Furthermore, spatial-temporal coordinates of physical objects make
possible the perception of a physical thing in different perceptual acts.
Different people can perceive physical objects at the same time because they
all perceive an object at the same place, it being a conceptual truth, says
Gale, that 'two material objects of the same kind cannot spatial-temporally
coincide' (Gale, 1994, p. 872).[1]

Lastly, a person can be said to perceive a numerically identical physical object at different times because there exists a contiguous spatial-temporal trail through which the object travels, giving content to the notion of its being the same object on different occasions.

Dimensionality, spatial-temporal location, therefore, gives content to the very notion of a physical perceptual particular. So, concludes Gale, by analogy if God too were to be a perceptual particular, God would have to have dimensionality, or at least something analogous to it. God does not have dimensionality or an analogue. Hence, God cannot be a perceptual particular.

What we have in perceptions of God, therefore, is nothing other than 'God-like' phenomenal particulars not backed up by a perceptual particular. Hence, no number of recurring experiences in which a subject reports perceiving God could cohere together to provide evidence that one being, God, was the subject of all these episodes. Indeed, not even in one instance could God be considered the object of the perception, since God cannot be an object of perception at all. If Gale's conceptual argument is correct, then the Argument from Perception collapses.

Reply to the Conceptual Argument

In reply, I note that while Gale is right that dimensionality would be sufficient to give meaning to the very notion of an object's existing unperceived, and thus fulfill Gale's first requirement, it is hardly necessary. In God's case, in particular, it is not necessary. After all, God is conceived of as having an inner life. Conceptually, to say that God exists when not perceived implies, then, that God's inner life continues when God is not perceived by anybody. That suffices to give content to the concept of God's continued existence unperceived, without having to place God into anything analogous to spatial-temporal coordinates. So, God passes Gale's first test that we must be able to understand what it means for God to exist when not perceived.

I am aware that some philosophers have objected to the notion of a being having an inner life while not possessing a body. They would not be swayed by my counter-argument. I need not argue that point here, though, because if those philosophers were right, this would show more than that God could not be a perceptual particular. It would show that no such reality as God could possibly exist. The point of the present argument, however, is not to show that God does not exist, but that if God were to exist, God could not be a perceptual particular, could not, that is, be an object of perception. An argument against God existing, on the other hand, lies beyond the scope of the present work. Therefore, I will simply bypass the stronger argument here and declare Gale's argument unsuccessful regarding the requirement that we understand what it would be for God to exist unperceived.

With regard to Gale's second requirement, that God must be able to be the common object of different perceptions in order for God to be a perceptual particular, we should remember that in order for an object just to *be* a common object of different perceptions, it is not necessary that anyone know that it is. That God has an inner life suffices to give conceptual content to the claim that God, in virtue of having an inner life not dependent on God's being perceived, is the common object of perceptions. The same holds for Gale's third requirement, that there be a distinction between numerical and qualitative identity. To possess the concept of God as numerically identical across perceptions, it is enough that we understand that an object possessing the same inner life is perceived on different occasions.

Therefore, Gale's 'conceptual argument' against the very idea of God's being a perceptual particular seems wanting.

Gale's Epistemological Argument

In the epistemological argument, Gale's idea is that unless it were possible for there to be *evidence* that an alleged object was the common object of different perceptual perceptions, one could not be justified in thinking one had perceived a substantive, perceptual particular rather than having experienced a mere phenomenal particular, private to one's own perception. For example, unless one could at least in principle fix a tree as the object of various perceptions, one could not be sure one had perceived a certain tree rather than having had mere 'treeish' perceptual experiences not backed up by a real tree. One could be justified in thinking that having such evidence was possible only if the allegedly perceived object purportedly had dimensionality. But, again, God lacks dimensionality. It follows that there could be no evidence in favor of perceiving God rather than merely experiencing a 'Goddish' phenomenal content.

Here is my orderly reconstruction of Gale's epistemological argument:

1   In order for a perception to count as evidence that a subject perceived an object, it must be possible for there to be evidence that the object in question is the common object of different perceptual perceptions.
2   It is possible for there to be evidence that an object is the common object of different perceptual perceptions only if it is possible to distinguish perceptions of that object from perceptions of (other) objects that are perceptually identical to it ('look' like it).
3   It is possible to distinguish perceptions of an object from perceptions of (other) objects that are perceptually identical to it, only if the object has dimensionality.
4   However, God does not have dimensionality.
5   Therefore, no perception can count as evidence that a subject has perceived God.

The epistemological argument presumes to regulate the *reidentification* of an object on more than one occasion. If we cannot apply the distinction between numerical identity and mere perceptual identity in practice, then we can have no evidence that what is now perceived is numerically identical with what is perceived on other occasions. Reidentification is possible only if the alleged perceptual particular exists in something at least analogous to space and time. Being in the same space at the same time implies numerical identity, as well as does a series of contiguous positions in space and time. Being in different spaces at the same time or lacking a series of contiguous positions in space and time implies numerical distinctness even if there is perceptual identity.

However, God does not exist in anything analogous to a space-time grid. Thus, there can never be evidence that what is perceived at two times is the same being: God.

If Gale were right, no number of perceptions of God, no matter how similar, could be sufficient to make possible the reidentification of God in perception. For since God does not exist in space, there is no way to have evidence that the same object, God, is being experienced, rather than an object perceptually similar but numerically distinct from God. There cannot be evidence even that it is probably the same object on different occasions, since there is no way of reckoning the probabilities when not having any way to distinguish between numerical and perceptual identity.

How much more telling is Gale's epistemological objection when the perceptual content of God-perceptions can differ from episode to episode, as pointed out in Chapter One. Why suppose these differing perceptions are all of one being? Dimensionality supplies the answer for physical objects. My pen with a scratch and without can be known to be the same pen because in principle I could trace a contiguous spatial-temporal route on which lie both the unscratched and scratched pens. God, alas, travels no contiguous spatial-temporal route, contiguous or otherwise.

Reply to the Epistemological Argument

I want to show that Gale's epistemological argument does not succeed in proving its conclusion. My response will be to point out that the argument is an unjustified 'skeptical' attack upon the possibility of perceiving God. This is because it unjustifiably rejects the possibility of there being a holistic practice specific to the reidentification of God, parallel to the holistic practice of reidentifying physical objects.

Reidentifying physical objects is 'holistic' in that we make the determination of the space an object occupies relative to reidentification of surrounding objects, while at the same time reidentification of surrounding objects depends on a judgment as to what space is occupied. As Peter Strawson has put it (1964, p. 37):

the identification and distinction of places turn on the identification and distinction of things; and the identification and distinction of things turn, in part, on the identification and distinction of places. There is no mystery about this mutual dependence. To exhibit its detail is simply to describe the criteria by which we criticize, amend and extend our ascription of identity to things and places.

Strawson goes on to describe our practice of reidentifying physical objects, in a way that uses the interplay between qualitative features and relative positions to determine both location and identity. The judgments we make are not empirically determined piece by piece. They reflect, rather, a holistic practice of making reidentifications.

An illustration of Strawson's point is when I decide that the streetlight in front of my house is the same one that was there yesterday. I do so in part because it occupies the same place as yesterday's streetlight. How do I decide, though, that I am looking at the same place as I did yesterday? I do so by reference to the place in question being in front of my same house, on the same stretch of the same street, and so on. However, the identification of the same house, stretch, and street, all depend upon determining they occupy the same place *they* occupied yesterday. Otherwise, for all I know, there is a house similar to mine in front of a street similar to mine somewhere else, and I am there, looking at a different streetlight from the one in front of my house. So, the identifications go around in a circle, from places to objects and from objects to places. However, the circle is not vicious since it represents a holistic practice of identifying together, as it were, spaces and objects.

It would not do, of course, to reply that it is very unlikely that there would be another house and another street so strikingly similar to mine, so that I could safely discount that hypothesis. We think we know that the hypothesis is unlikely, after all, based on our employment of the holistic practice of physical object identification. The present point is that without that practice in place we could not have built up the probabilities in question.

Now there is no obvious reason why the reidentification of God cannot take place within its own holistic practice, with its own criteria of identification, not beholden to the practice involved in reidentifying physical objects. We are not obligated to link the very notion of having evidence for a perceptual particular to the specific holistic practice of reidentifying physical objects, or something analogous. To refuse to acknowledge this is not an argument against the possibility of God's reidentification in perception, but a merely skeptical stance towards that possibility.

Strawson's world of sounds   It will be instructive to compare what I am claiming for perceptions of God to Peter Strawson's 'world of sounds'. In the second chapter of his *Individuals*, Strawson presents a scheme in which a subject locates objective sound particulars according to their 'position' as determined by the gradually changing pitch of what Strawson calls the 'master-sound'. Being heard together with a certain pitch of the master-sound fixes the location of a sound without the aid of any spatial features. Different locations at the master-sound yield distinct sound particulars. Strawson thus provides a way of distinguishing between numerical and qualitative identity in a purely auditory world, based on the pitch of the master-sound. Here is part of Strawson's description of his world of sounds (Strawson, 1964, p. 77):

> Suppose ... a certain unitary sound-sequence, to which we may refer as M (M being the name of a universal) is being heard at a certain pitch-level of the master-sound – say at level L. Then suppose the master-sound changes fairly rapidly in pitch to Level L′ and back again to L; and then M is heard once more, a few bars having been missed. Then the sound-particular now being heard is reidentified as the same particular instance of M. If during the same time, the master-sound had changed not from L to L′ and back to L, but from L to L″, then even though M may have been heard once more, a few bars having been missed, it is not the same particular instance of M that is now heard, but a different instance.

In this scheme, qualitatively identical sounds are distinguished by their relationship to the pitch of the master-sound. Sounds at the same pitch of the master-sound are numerically identical to one another, even if not phenomenally the same (the tune has advanced a few bars). Sounds are numerically distinct, if they are at different pitches of the master-sound, no matter how similar they are phenomenally. Now, if perceptual sound particulars can be numerically reidentified without benefit of space, then space is not required to apply the distinction between numerical and qualitative identity for perceptual particulars. In that case, God too could be a perceptual particular even though there exists no analogue of spatial position for God. Reidentification of God would follow its own scheme of identification just as does Strawson's world of sounds.

Gale criticizes Strawson's treatment of sounds. Here is the problem as Gale sees it. The position of every sound, S, other than the master-sound, is determined by the pitch of the master-sound along with which S is heard. It is the difference in the pitch of the master-sound between when S is heard and when S′ is heard that determines that S and S′ are numerically distinct even if S and S′ are perceptually identical, that is, sound the same. However, counter-argues Gale, S and S′ are never perceptually similar in such situations, because they have different perceptual relational properties, namely being heard at different pitches of the master-sound. Pitch is a perceptual quality, and relations to that quality are perceptually discernible. Hence, in Strawson's scheme each distinct sound has a distinct phenomenal quality, so that each case of perceptual qualitative identity must yield numerical identity. The case is different for spatial objects, since being in a certain space is not a perceptual quality of an object. Space is not an empirically detected realm.

Perhaps I can put Gale's objection to Strawson a bit differently. With spatial particulars, it makes sense to think of a particular changing place. However, Strawson's sounds cannot change place. Strawson declares that if S and S′ are perceptually identical they are nevertheless numerically distinct if they are heard at different pitches of the master-sound. But, we may ask, why can't the same sound move from being heard at one pitch of the master-sound to being heard at another pitch of the master-sound? The answer is that the distinctness of sounds is guaranteed by the perceptual quality of being heard at different pitches of the master-sound. This leaves no room for the idea of the same sound moving about on the pitch scale of the master-sound. If that is so, then we really do not have a concept of a sound as a perceptual particular, since we have no way of giving conceptual content to the numerical distinction between perceptually identical sounds. Strawson has not given us a non-spatial explication of a perceptual particular. So, Strawson's world of sounds is of no help as a counter to Gale.

Now, Strawson is well aware that there are disanalogies between his individuation of sounds and the individuation of physical objects in space. One disanalogy he mentions is that in the world of sounds one cannot hear different sounds together as located by the master-sound, whereas we can apprehend distinct spatial objects together. Another disanalogy we might mention is that the locations of sounds, that is to say pitches of the master-sound, are not determined holistically. The master-sound is simply given, *as* the master-sound. Spatial locations, which aid in identifying physical objects, on the other hand, are identified only holistically. Other disanalogies have been pointed out as well (see Glouberman, 1975).

In this connection, Strawson declares that there is no over-arching standard by which to determine whether his sounds are 'really' objective particulars (Strawson, 1964, p. 81). Strawson writes of his scheme of sounds (p. 77):

> The resultant conceptual scheme ... is not compelling. We could adopt a different scheme ... which allowed for reidentifiable universals but not for reidentifiable particulars. What we cannot do is, as it were, to appear to accept a scheme which allows for reidentification of sound-particulars and then to say that, of course, particular-identity would always be in doubt ... This would be the position of philosophical scepticism about the identity of sound particulars.

Strawson's point is that a person could refuse to adopt a conceptual scheme in which particular sounds were reidentified as they are in his sound world, and insist, for example, on speaking only of reinstantiations of 'sound-universals'. But of course we could just as well insist on something comparable for our ordinary world of physical objects. We could, if we chose, adopt an ontology in which there were only universals and their instantiations, or in which there were only physical processes, ruling out abiding perceptual physical particulars altogether. The reidentification practice we employ lacks compulsion. Hence, the holistic identification of Strawson's sounds is really no worse off than the holistic identification of physical objects.

Now, I have no stake in defending the soundness of Strawson's example of his world of sounds. What does interest me, rather, is his insight that there can very well be different conceptual systems, each giving different criteria for perceptual particular-hood in that system. If so, the possibility remains that the reidentification of God occurs in a holistic identifying practice that is no less respectable than the one in place for reidentifying physical objects.

In order to strengthen this point, let us look at some of the more important objections that philosophers have raised to Strawson's treatment of sound particulars, and see whether they might apply to the case of God. Strawson himself questions the coherence of an objective purely auditory world because observers would have a concept of themselves at a certain place and so possess spatial concepts. However, my concern is not with whether there can be an observer who possesses no spatial concepts, who possesses nonetheless the concept of a non-spatial perceptual particular. For my purposes, it is sufficient if we can possess a concept of a specific kind of perceptual particular and identify it without importing our spatial concepts into the understanding of it. So this objection to Strawson's point would not be relevant to us.

In a penetrating discussion of Strawson's chapter on sounds, Gareth Evans raised some important criticisms of Strawson (Evans, 1980). Firstly, Evans argued that Strawson's sound scheme is open to a phenomenalist reduction, that is, to saying merely that 'if the master-sound were at pitch l, then a sound of a certain sort would be heard', at pitch 1, rather than that there was a substantive, enduring sound particular heard when the master-sound was at pitch l. Secondly, Evans argues that Strawson could not distinguish empirically between objective sound 'particulars' and objective sound 'processes' in his scheme. That is, Strawson's scheme is not powerful enough to ensure that what was heard at a given pitch of the master-sound was a particular and not a process. Evans thus drives a wedge between 'objectivity', applying to both particulars and processes, and particularity.

Thirdly, Evans argued that we could not conceive of sounds as perceptual particulars at all, since sounds give only secondary, perceptual qualities, volume, pitch, timbre, and the like, and not primary, enduring qualities. As Evans puts it: '*We* can think of sounds as ... phenomena that are independent of us, and that can exist unperceived because we have the resources for thinking of the abiding stuff in whose changes the truth of the proposition that there is a sound can be regarded as consisting' (p. 104). To get a perceptual particular in a world of sounds, declares Evans, we must import an enduring physical object that emits the sound. The sound is then identified as the one coming from that object. Minus such an object, Strawson's world of sounds fails to supply reidentifications of sounds.

None of these objections by Evans applies to perceptions of God. As noted earlier, the perception of God is commonly a perception of a reality possessed of an enduring inner life. This makes difficult any phenomenalist reduction of God's appearances. It counts against reducing God to mere possibilities of our having perceptions of a certain kind. For the same reason, perceptions of God make difficult an interpretation of God as a process rather than a particular. Finally, even if we were to restrict ourselves to secondary properties of God, such perceptions suggest that the substance that has these secondary properties has an enduring inner life. In God's case, we need not posit a spatial particular in which the secondary properties abide.

One point made by Evans, and by Jonathan Bennett (1966, p. 37), that is relevant to perceptions of God is that Strawson could have made do without the master-sound altogether (Evans, 1980, pp. 81–2). In place of the master-sound Strawson could have suggested a sufficient regularity of perceptions that supported generalizations of the form: 'A perception of kind 1 will intervene between any perception of kinds 2 and 3.' In the resulting scheme intervening perceptions would be regarded as objective interruptions between perceptions of the same object. This scheme would provide subjects with a holistic way to generate the notion of reidentifiable particulars. This could have been done without any master-sound. Put differently, intervening perceptions could grant subjects the notion of a 'block' accounting for their not perceiving a perceptual particular on a particular occasion. The explanation for its non-perception would be that something was blocking its being perceived, as when a truck passes by a park bench and blocks it from view from across the street.

Interestingly, something analogous to Evans' suggestion is possible in the case of perceptions of God. Since God is alleged to have an inner life it is possible for there to be a series of occurrences that could be attributed to a series of events in God's inner life. For example, on one occasion it seems that God is promising to do A, and on another occasion it seems that God is telling someone that God has brought about A, and so on. This could give a sequence that a subject could attribute to a particular that persists between perceptions. This is especially possible if the subject had a sense at times of something blocking the having of a perception of God. Such a block can be found in the idea that the possibility of one's experiencing God depends upon overcoming one's egocentric predicament to a significant degree, moving away from being the center of one's ultimate concern, and opening oneself to God. An inability to do so would tend to block one's ability to be aware of God's presence. Of course, we would have to apply the patterns of perception and the blocks together in a holistic way. However, in that, as we have seen, there would be nothing out of the ordinary.

I conclude that, in principle, for perceptions of God there could be a holistic reidentification practice parallel to Evans' reidentification practice for perceptual sound particulars *sans* anything analogous to a master-sound. Therefore, with or without the master-sound, Gale's epistemological objection fails for not having recognized the possibilities of different holistic schemes in which we could have evidence for the existence of non-spatial perceptual particulars.

Reidentifying God

I would not like to stop there, however. All I have argued is that, in principle, there could be a reidentification practice for perceptions of God. And while that may be sufficient to turn back the epistemological argument, which says that in principle there could not be a reidentification practice, this says little about the actual possibilities of reidentifying God in perception. The question I now want to ask, then, is this: What would be the phenomenal features in perceptions of God, in mystical traditions and without, that would play a determining role in reidentifying the object of the perceptions as one perceptual particular, God, as opposed to a multiplicity of similar-seeming particulars?

Several supporting features come to mind: the seeming constancy of God's character in the mainstream of mystical traditions, and the existence of perceptions of God of a serial nature, suggesting a being enduring between perceptions. Add to these the phenomenon of 'auto-identification', where God identifies God's self to the subject of the experience, as the same one who appeared to others, or to the same subject at a different time. Of course, these do not prove that the same reality appears across perceptions. Nonetheless, they contribute to a rationale for reidentification.

These supporting features support one particular feature I believe should play a major role in reidentification of God. I will describe this aspect of theistic perception from Jewish sources, with which I am most familiar, though it figures as a feature in other mystical and religious traditions. Beginning at least in the Tannaitic era (the first two centuries of the present era) God gets referred to as 'The Place' (*HaMakom*). For example, a Mishnah states: 'Rabbi Shimon says, "When you pray do not make your prayer routine, but supplication for mercy before The Place, Blessed be He"' (*Avot*, Chapter Two, Mishnah 13).[2] And a Midrash says: 'Blessed is The Place, Blessed be He, who knows all from beginning to end ... and in His wisdom and understanding created His world and prepared it and afterwards created Adam ...' (*Eliyahu Rabbah*, Section A).[3]

The later Amoratic literature contains several passages that give an interpretation of the name 'The Place', as in this representative text (*Genesis Rabbah*, Section 68):

> Rabbi Huna said in the name of Rabbi Ami: Why is the Holy One Blessed Be He called by the name 'The Place'? Because He is the place of the world and His world is not His place. So it is written, 'Behold place is with me' (Exodus 33:21) to tell us that He is the place of the world and His world is not His place.

The proof text in Exodus, reading in the King James version: 'there is a place by me', appears where Moses asks to see God's presence and God passes God's glory before him. Moses sees only God's back. He does not see God, because God has no place. God, according to the above Midrash, is The Place of the world.[4]

This statement has been given a mystical reading in Jewish sources: that the world is, somehow, included within the reality of God, and God is not 'in' the world. Understood as a mystical pronouncement, that God was the Place of the world served as a prototype for mystical ideas of the later Jewish kabbalah, such as that the Infinite One contracted to its 'sides' to make 'room' for the creation. The creation then came into being in the 'space' vacated inside the Infinite One. God, then, is the place of the world in the sense that the world exists in the 'emptied' space inside God.

Maimonides, the arch rationalist, gave a non-mystical understanding of the term 'place' when used of God. He writes (Maimonides, 1963, Part One, Chapter Eight, p. 33):

> *Place* [*makom*]. Originally this term was given the meaning of particular and general place. Subsequently, language extended its meaning and made it a term denoting an individual's rank and situation; I mean to say with reference to his perfection in some matter, so it is said: *A certain man has a certain place* with regard to a certain matter. You know how often the people of our language use this meaning when they say: *Occupying the place of his ancestors; He occupied the place of his ancestors in wisdom or piety*; ... It is in this figurative manner that it is said: *Blessed be the glory of the Lord from His place* (Ezek. 3:12), meaning according to His rank and the greatness of His portion in existence. Similarly in every mention of *place* referring to God, the sole intention is to signify the rank of His existence, may He be exalted; there being nothing like or similar to that existence, as shall be demonstrated.

According to Maimonides, then, when used of God, '*makom*' has an evaluational meaning. So, calling God *HaMakom*, 'The Place', would be asserting God's incomparable status or 'place' in the order of things. 'The Place', for Maimonides, refers to the supremely valuable reality. Taking the hint from Maimonides, I suggest that calling God 'The Place of the world' has implications for the reidentification practice attached to perceptions of God.

Remember that, in Strawson's sound world, the master-sound determines the identity of every other sound. Yet, the location, and hence the identity, of the master-sound is not determined by anything. In fact, the master-sound has no location in Strawson's world of sounds. Its identity as the master-sound is simply a given in the conceptual scheme. All else is measured by it. The role of the master-sound in the world of sounds simply does not allow for such questions as 'Is that still the master-sound?' or, 'Is that the master-sound again?' to arise. Alternatively, the systemic role the master-sound plays in the world of sounds, that of determiner of all other sounds, holistically determines reidentification of the master-sound. 'Is that still the master-sound?' receives an answer simply by pointing to the way the world of sounds works.

Analogously, as a feature of perceptions of God, perceiving God as 'The Place' of the world implies perceiving something as being not just another particular within a scheme of particulars, but as that in reference to which all particulars have their existence and find their value. This is not just a conceptual claim, but also a phenomenal report of (at least) well-developed God-perceptions.[5] To say that God is *HaMakom*, 'The Place' of the world, is to make God the 'master-sound', as it were, of the world. I am suggesting, then, that the reidentification of God across perceptions can take place within a practice that recognizes an ontological-valuational center around which all existence becomes organized and understood. The question of whether it is the same center from occasion to occasion just does not arise. In the 'practice' being considered, it just *is* the same center. That is just the way God functions in the conceptual scheme attached to perceptions of God.

Alternatively, to determine whether subjects perceived the same reality in different perceptions of God, it would be enough to describe a holistic practice in which those perceptions played a role. Whether one experienced the same ontological-valuational center or a different one, is decided by the holistic practice in which perceptions of God occur. The practice determines that it is God in all cases.

Nothing I have said is supposed to *prove* that subjects perceive one object, namely God, rather than distinct, though similar objects, in perceptions of God. Rather my point is that the reidentification practice for God can be radically different from the reidentification practice for physical objects. In that event, Gale's epistemological argument fails for not having appreciated the distinctive context of theistic perceptions. We need not agree, therefore, that to be justified in thinking that different subjects were perceiving (the same) God, God must have dimensionality.

I conclude that Gale's epistemological argument fails to show that there could not be evidence from perception for the existence of God.

My position should not be confused with what sometimes has been called a 'fideistic' approach.[6] In the latter, the practice of taking certain kinds of perceptual inputs as 'of-God' would have its own 'logic' and justification conditions that were not beholden to any criteria outside of the circle of the practice itself. Hence, the question of justifying a belief that God is genuinely experienced could not arise.

This is not my position. I am not arguing that the mere existence of the practice of taking experiences as genuine perceptions of God justifies giving it credence. On the other hand, it would be a mistake, and here is my point, to insist on holding perceptions of God to identification procedures, or their analogue, appropriate for physical object identifications, procedures obviously not appropriate elsewhere. Why should we? I have shown that this is required neither conceptually nor epistemologically.

Granted, a person could refuse to recognize a valid identification practice like the one I am suggesting for God-perceptions. However, that would have little to support it in the way of argument. I admit, though, that, because of that possibility, the Argument from Perception is not rationally compelling, in the sense of obligating just everyone to its conclusion. The phenomenon of perceptions of God will lack evidential sufficiency for those who do not acknowledge the accompanying identification conditions. The most a defender of the Argument from Perception can hope for, therefore, is a line of reasoning that can be held (only) by some in a rational way that confers evidential sufficiency on the phenomenon of perceptions of God. This, however, is not an earth-shaking concession. Similar restrictions apply to trying to show that this is the same pen that was here yesterday. Someone who acknowledges only a pen-universal and its momentary instantiations, say, rather than enduring physical pens, will not be convinced by any story dependent on the holistic practice of physical object identification.

The moral of the story is that Gale has provided a possible reason for why some person might not go along with the Argument from Perception, but has not provided a cogent argument against it.

Notes

1   There may be a problem here. Perhaps there could be two distinct yet phenomenally indistinct objects, O1 and O2. Jones senses O1 at place p at time t, and Smith senses O2 at the same place, at the same time. There is no incoherence in this. Jones has a perceptual apparatus that senses at p at t objects that are really ten degrees to the left, while Smith has a perceptual apparatus that senses objects ten degrees to the right. The objects do not exist in the same place but are perceived at the same place at the same time. If there were such systematic distortions there could be a phenomenally identical perception of distinct objects at the same spatial-temporal coordinate, making it impossible for us to know whether we had to do with one or many objects.

2   Translations from Hebrew texts are mine.

3   The late Judaic scholar Efraim Aurbach argued that *HaMakom*, 'The Place', occurs in contrast to calling God, 'shamayim', or 'Heaven'. God is called 'The Place', accordingly, when God's nearness is being emphasized, and is called 'Heaven' when God is thought of as distant (Aurbach, 1975, Chapter 4). However, nowhere does the Tannaitic literature explain the term.

4   Aurbach, 1975, maintains that this interpretation of 'The Place' is a departure from an earlier understanding. His thinking is that in earlier times when the Rabbis were in Palestine, *HaMakom* was a way of referring to God's presence at a certain place, the Temple. When the Temple was no longer standing, the Rabbis wanted to weaken the connection between God and a particular place. I do not find this proposal convincing. The Amoratic Rabbis taught regularly that it was the *shekhinah*, God's 'immanent presence', rather than God Himself that rested on the Temple, and in the Amoratic literature the *shekhinah* continues to have a place, at the Temple site, or in exile with the Jewish people, or filling the world. In addition, they generally kept the *shekhinah* separate from *HaMakom*, as when a Midrash says that '*HaMakom* showed the *shekhinah* to Ezekial' (*Seder Olam Rabbah*, Chapter 26). Whether or not the later teachers knew the original significance of the name *HaMakom*, I suggest they meant to distinguish

between the *shekhinah*, which they thought of as a localized manifestation of God, and God. The *shekhinah* can have a place. God cannot.

5   Paul Helm, 2000, questions whether perceptions of God could have such a phenomenal content, but concedes that 'perhaps' they do.

6   In private correspondence, Richard Gale has so characterized my position.

Chapter 4

Alternative Explanations I: The Alternative Explanation Response

The 'Alternative Explanation Response', as I shall call it, to the Argument from Perception contends that always, or for the most part, persons who seem to have alleged experiences of God are in circumstances generating alternative naturalistic explanations that nullify or weaken the initial evidential sufficiency of God-perceptions. An explanation of perceptions of God is an 'alternative', then, relative to the 'theistic explanation' for why it seems that God appears to a person, namely that God really *is* appearing to that person.

This chapter is dedicated to explaining two different forms of the Alternative Explanation Response. The first I will call the 'reductionist' form, and exists when specific naturalistic explanations are advanced for theistic mystical experiences. It is an attempt to transfer the explanation of mystical experiences of God from the supernatural to the natural realm by supplying a good naturalistic explanation. The reductionist need not maintain that just one type of relevant naturalistic circumstance typically obtains, such as being in a pathological condition or being under the influence of drugs. The circumstances may be disjunctive, that is, there may be several types of circumstances involved, where each person who seems to experience God is in one or another of them. The reductionist deems a person's being in one or another of these circumstances a good, alternative explanation for why they experienced God.

The second form I will call the 'disappearance theory of God-perceptions' or simply 'the disappearance theory' form of the Alternative Explanation Response. The disappearance theory does not have specific naturalistic conditions to point to as an explanation. Instead it contends that God should disappear from our explanation, since in principle we should reject supernatural explanations, whether or not we possess a viable naturalistic alternative. On this view, then, whatever explanations might turn out to be adequate will be naturalistic ones, and God will not figure in them.

Typically, scientists and philosophers advance reductionist explanations after having already discounted, at least by implication, the theistic explanation of perceptions of God. Their research programs seek an explanation for what in their eyes would otherwise lack an explanation. They are not engaged in giving a response to the claim of initial evidential sufficiency. Presumably, those volunteering alternatives either think there are good, prior reasons for thinking God is not perceived, or take it on faith that the theistic explanation lacks justification. Indeed, they might subscribe to the disappearance theory of mystical experiences of God.

I am not addressing reductionist explanations in that way. My enterprise consists of examining alternative explanations as a reason for denying the initial evidential sufficiency of perceptions of God. I am not examining which alternative explanations might be the best, when supposing theistic experiences are deluded. On the contrary, I am endorsing the Argument from Perception and am assuming that an impressive number of perceptions of God enjoy initial evidential sufficiency. That means that an alternative explanation of perceptions of God will have to make a serious dent in the initial credibility of the theistic explanation.

Reductionism

Within the reductionist form of the Alternative Explanation Response, I distinguish two approaches. One approach I will call 'evidence-reductionism', and the second 'truth-reductionism'.[1] Evidence reductionism, or 'e-reductionism', says there is a set of naturalistic circumstances in which perceptions of God occur, which generate alternative explanations that give good reason for abandoning the initial evidential sufficiency of God-perceptions. Evidence reductionism wishes no more than to undermine the initial evidential value of perceptions of God. As far as its claims go, people might have valid perceptions of God. The only problem is that we have no good evidence that they do. E-reductionism does not claim to be able to show perceptions of God to be illusory, only under-supported as for genuineness.

E-reductionists need not claim that *all* subjects who perceive God are in the e-reductionist explanation-providing circumstances. They need find only a sufficient number of cases to credibly weaken the initial evidential sufficiency of perceptions of God. I will shorten this requirement to a claim about 'most' occurrences of God-perceptions, though we might very well require more than just a majority of cases.

E-reductionism, then, bases itself on the following sort of claim:

(E) There is a set of naturalistic circumstances C, such that most subjects who perceive God are in some C-circumstance (that is, are in some circumstance included in C), and being in some C-circumstance is a reason to expect or suspect those subjects would have had God-perceptions, even if their perceptions were illusory.

In (E), to say that being in a C-circumstance is a reason to 'expect' subjects would have (thought they) perceived God, is to claim that we could have predicted on naturalistic grounds alone that subjects who had mystical experiences of God were going to have them. To say that being in a C-

circumstance is a reason to 'suspect' they would have (thought they) perceived God is to make a weaker claim. It is to assert that perhaps we could
not have predicted a mystical experience of God beforehand, but once it
occurs we can discover naturalistic reasons that could explain its occurrence, even if it were illusory. We could find a plausible causal story explaining why they experienced what they did.

To illustrate, suppose we discovered that most God-perceivers were af-
flicted with a dreadful case of infantile regression. They craved a father or
mother image. Suppose we also knew how regressive anxieties might (not:
'do') cause people to have all sorts of hallucinations. Then we would have
reason to suspect that people who perceived God might have done so even if
their experiences were illusory. They might have experienced 'God-images'
even were God not appearing to them. We would not have been able to
predict they would but, once they had such experiences, we should be alert
for the likelihood of false sightings.

E-reductionism finds stronger support in expectations than in suspicions.
Nonetheless, both expectations and suspicions would count against the initial evidential case for the theistic explanation. The e-reductionist claims
that, since in most perceptions of God we would have expected or suspected
the subjects would have their experiences even if undergoing illusions, the
mere fact that subjects had such experiences would count little or not at all
toward their veracity.

'Truth reductionism', or 't-reductionism', goes further. It proposes that
perceptions of God occur in a set of naturalistic circumstances that generate
good reasons for rejecting perceptions of God as genuine – for saying that
subjects do not have veridical God-perceptions. T-reductionism denies the
very truth of the theistic explanation, not only the evidential case for its
validity.

T-reductionists might want to claim that all perceptions of God were
illusory but, in the context of our inquiry, they need not go so far. I construe
t-reductionism as including the position that most God-perceptions were
illusory and those that might be authentic, for all we know, just were not
numerous enough to provide the cohering evidential support required by the
Argument from Perception. That is, t-reductionists could recognize an insignificant number of God-perceptions that might be, for all we know, authentic, without acknowledging that the phenomenon of theistic perceptions had
evidential sufficiency. T-reductionism will have succeeded if it could show
we were left with an insignificant number of God-perceptions unexplained
by the t-reductionist favored alternative explanations. I will sum up this
requirement as being about 'most' perceptions of God. In sum, t-reductionism
makes this claim:

(T) There is a set of naturalistic circumstances C, such that most subjects who
perceive God are in some C-circumstance, and being in some C-circumstance is
a reason to believe or suspect those subjects had illusory God-perceptions.

Here is the kind of argument t-reductionists might employ to establish (T). They would start with claiming that there was a set of naturalistic circumstances C, such that most subjects who perceive God are in some C-circumstance. Then they would advance to the claim that it was not plausible that most subjects who veridically perceived God would be in some C-circumstance. Therefore, it was not plausible to suppose that perceptions of God were veridical. So in all likelihood they were not veridical.

Here is an illustration: Suppose we discovered that most people who had mystical experiences of God had taken mescaline before their experiences. The t-reductionist might argue that this makes it entirely unlikely that these people had really encountered God. It simply does not square with God's supposed character to think God would appear only to people who had taken mescaline. Nothing singles out mescaline users for the special treatment implied by their having really experienced God. Furthermore, they might argue, as Robert Oakes has, that if a person were to genuinely perceive God that would be a consequence of God's initiative rather than of a person's 'making' God appear (Oakes, 1976).[2] Hence, people who seemed to perceive God (who are all mescaline takers) most likely did not have veridical perceptions of God.

Now, to make their case, a reductionist of either the e- or t- variety would start by determining the relevant naturalistic circumstances, the set C, that most persons who perceive God are in. Next, the reductionist would show that being in those circumstances was causally related to the having of theistic mystical experiences. The reductionist will have to defend a causal statement to the effect that whenever (or generally when) a person is in a C-circumstance, this will (probably) cause the person to have a God-perception, or that this should at least make us suspect as much. For example, a reductionist might insist that generally when people seem to experience God they have an overwhelming desire to have such experiences. Furthermore, the reductionist would argue that the psychological need would (probably) cause people to have the mystical experiences. The psychological need will be offered as the cause of their mystical episodes, as backed up, say, by a well-established theory about psychological needs and subsequent experiences.

This would not be enough, however. A reductionist would have to show as well that being in the C-circumstance in question was not, in addition, a reason to think that perceptions of God in that circumstance would be veridical. Otherwise, the reductionist would fail to show that in the C-circumstance in question a subject would have perceived God even were that perception illusory. Here is the idea. Suppose we discovered that everyone who had theistic perceptions had a deep psychological need to experience God. Suppose, further, a reductionist offered this as the cause of the experience, subjects' desires being so great that they unconsciously generated the experience for themselves, and would have done so whether or not God was actually appearing to them. This argument would not yet undercut the evidence for thinking subjects had veridical God-perceptions, since it

might be that people's strong desire to experience God was answered by
God actually appearing to them. If so, that a person was in the said psychological state would not undercut the initial case for the validity of God-
perceptions. To be successful, the reductionist's C-circumstance must not
give us reason to think a God-perception was indeed veridical.

Even that is not enough. Because mystical experiences of God occur
under such widely varying personal and cultural circumstances, to be persuasive the reductionist should give us reason to think the following
implausible: That there exists a set of naturalistic circumstances, C1, in
addition to C, such that most persons who seem to perceive God are in a C1-
circumstance, and that being in a C1-circumstance was a good reason to
think they would have authentic God-perceptions. The point is this: suppose
we could determine some set of naturalistic circumstances C in which most
perceptions of God took place, and we knew that being in a C-circumstance
was a good reason for expecting a person to perceive God even if the
perception were illusory. This would seriously contest the initial evidential
sufficiency of God-perceptions only if there were no further set of naturalistic
circumstances, C1, such that people who perceived God were in a C1
circumstance and C1 gave good reason to think God was really perceived.
In other words, the reductionist must give us at least some reason to believe
that no C1-circumstances re-support the theistic explanation.[3]

To illustrate, suppose we discovered – let this be naturalistic circumstances C – that most subjects who reported perceptions of God had been
longing to experience God. Suppose further we had a well-grounded causal
generalization from desiring unusual experiences to the having of them,
from which we could infer that people in the given C-circumstance probably
would have, or might have had, mystical experiences of God even if illusory. We would then have succeeded in fulfilling the previous reductionist
conditions for weakening the initial evidential case for theistic experiences.
However, we would not thereby have convincingly weakened the evidence
for the veridicality of theistic experiences. For suppose the same people
who had mystical experiences of God were also in some further circumstances, let this be our C1 circumstances. For example, they all had undergone years of serous spiritual training, their histories showed that even
though they had many desires for unusual experiences, they, as opposed to
most people in similar situations, rarely made claims based on their desires
to have unusual experiences; that they were level-headed, sober, conservative folk, and so on. This would restore the evidential value of perceptions
of God and would invalidate the force of discovering these subjects had
been in the proclaimed C-circumstance when perceiving God. The point is
that since the phenomenon of experiencing God mystically is spread across
history, cultures and religions, we would have a right to suspect that maybe
a cited C-circumstance was not the whole story.

In order to undermine convincingly the initial evidential sufficiency of
perceptions of God, reductionists should be able to give reasons for thinking

there were no such additional circumstances supportive of the theistic explanation of perceptions of God. We would want to know quite a bit more
about the subjects before judging counter-indicative circumstances to be
enough.

To sum up, the reductionist claim (R) should include all of the following:

(a)   There is a set of naturalistic circumstances C, such that most (perhaps
       all) subjects who perceive God are in some C-circumstance.
(b)   Being in a C-circumstance gives reason to expect or suspect those
       subjects would have had God perceptions, even if their perceptions
       were illusory (e-reductionism), or being in a C-circumstance gives
       reason to expect or suspect those subjects had illusory God-perceptions
       (t-reductionism).
(c)   There is no set C1 of naturalistic circumstances, such that: most sub-
       jects who perceive God are in some C1-circumstance and being in a
       C1-circumstance counts significantly in favor of the subjects having
       had veridical experiences of God.

and:

(d)   A person's being in C does not give reason to expect or suspect the
       person's perceptions would be veridical, if God existed.

Reductionist Strategies

Enumeration   Reductionists have available two possible strategies for
grounding their reductionist program, as expressed in (R). Regarding clause
(a), the first would be to employ a generalization from an enumeration of
known cases to the conclusion that (a) was true. The second would be to
motivate accepting (a) theoretically. This would be accomplished by arguing
against the theistic explanation of God-perceptions on theoretical grounds,
in favor of a theory saying what would be plausible C-circumstances for (a).

The first strategy might depend on documentation of God-perceptions by
subjects suffering from pathological conditions, such as severe deprivation,
severe sexual frustration, intense fear of death, pronounced maladjustment or
mental illness. Then the strategy would generalize from those cases to get (a),
and proceed to argue for (b)–(d) of the reductionist position. As noted in an
earlier chapter, I have argued (Gellman, 1997), as has Caroline Franks Davis
(1989), that this strategy fails for reductionist attempts of this sort. A major
problem is in the generalization from the documented cases to (a) as conclusion. While alternative explanations do seem to a degree to whittle down the
sample-class of evidence for the authenticity of God-perceptions, a generalization from these cases to (a) is weakly supported. After all, the phenomenon
of God-perceptions includes garden variety, otherwise ordinary folk like you
and me, who have God-perceptions in prayer, contemplation and the like, and

in the course of their daily lives. What is more, a look at mystical traditions will reveal plenty of professional mystics who seem quite free of pathological conditions (as well as some who are not). I am afraid that the more titillating cases of God-perceivers more readily catch researchers' eyes and keyboards. This is hardly a basis for an empirical generalization. Of course, I am in no position to claim to be able to show that most God-perceivers are free of pathological troubles. We have no choice but to exercise common sense, based on what is known about the history of mystical traditions and the anthologies of reports of God-perceptions by novice mystics.

A second problem here is that it is an open question whether pathological conditions constituting the C-circumstances of the alternatives fulfill the conditions of clause (d) that a person's being in C does not give reason to expect the person will have veridical experiences of God, if God exists. People suffering greatly inwardly might be just the kind of people God would grace with a sense of the living Divine presence. An experience of God would be comforting and reassuring and could help a person to begin leading a happier, more fulfilled life.

Other alternative explanations that might try to generalize from enumerated cases, might point to non-pathological causes, such as hypersuggestibility, infantile regression, wish fulfillment or a religious psychological set. The main problem here is that it is far from clear that any of these could be expected or even suspected of causing God-perceptions. For example, while wish fulfillment certainly influences people, how often does it cause them to see perceptual apparitions? In addition, how often does a psychological set do so? Not often, indeed. I refer the reader to my previous discussion, and to Caroline Franks Davis, for the details of the arguments against such reductionist approaches.

Why have researchers been quick to move from documented, problematic God-perceivers to a generalization like (a)? Because, as I have already noted, usually researchers offer alternative explanations from the implicit assumption that the theistic explanation of God-perceptions should be rejected. If so, the evidential demands for alternative explanations become lowered. Since the loss of the theistic explanation leaves them high and dry, a somewhat speculative explanation starts to look attractive. However, begin with an initial evidential case for the theistic explanation, as we do here, and they will need better empirical grounding to make their alternative case.

Theoretical Advantages   The second reductionist strategy proceeds from theoretical reasons why we should prefer other explanations to the theistic one. Noting documented cases, these strategies would argue that explanations pointed to there, bear theoretical advantages over a theistic explanation of God-perceptions. So, we should adopt alternative explanations, at least provisionally.

On this approach, of two explanations we are to choose the one accounting for a wider array of empirical findings than the other, everything else being equal. For example, a theory accounting for both the motion of objects on earth and the motion of heavenly bodies is preferable to one that explains motion on earth alone. The former is a better theory than the latter. Correspondingly, the main theoretical advantage to be gained by alternative explanations lies in their capability to explain a far wider array of empirical findings than can the theistic explanation.

Here is an example of this strategy. Suppose we discovered that strikingly similar brain abnormalities were involved in a promising number of theistic perceptions and psychotic perceptions, respectively, and that we knew psychotic perceptions to be hallucinatory. A theory explaining both theistic and psychotic perceptions solely as hallucinatory products of that kind of brain abnormality would be better than maintaining two theories, one for psychotic experiences and a second for theistic ones. Everything else being equal, one comprehensive theory is better than two local ones.

On this approach, the question whether apparent theistic experiences are to be compared to psychotic ones, or to spirit-possession, or whatever, is not a matter for a priori insistence or rejection. All will depend on the advantage of wider explanatory power. If comparing theistic episodes to psychotic ones yields good results in terms of the scope of our theories, then that is the thing to do. If not, then perhaps not.

Whether this form of reductionism succeeds will depend much on the particular explanation advanced as well as upon the relevant empirical data. It would be absurd, for example, to deny that I ever really see anything with my eyes, because (suppose) my brain can be stimulated to make me think I see things when I do not. Concluding that whenever I think I am seeing something it is exclusively an internal activity of my brain and nervous system would have clear theoretical advantages: it would explain both the brain stimulation cases as well as the apparent sense-perception cases. However, that advantage would not be sufficient to deny we ever see physical objects in the world.

The two reductionist strategies, enumerative and theoretical, may of course be combined to support a specific proposal to replace the theistic explanation with a non-theistic one.

This closes my exposition of the reductionist form of the Alternative Explanation Response. In the following chapter, I present three representative reductionist theories, one sociological and two neuropsychological alternatives for the explanation of theistic mystical experiences.

The Disappearance Theory of God-perceptions

On the disappearance theory form of the Alternative Explanation Response, in principle we should reject the theistic explanation of God-perceptions, whether or not we possess a specific viable alternative. I call it the 'disappearance theory', because it presents reasons why God, in effect, should disappear from our explanations for theistic-type experiences. The disappearance theory differs from reductionism in invoking a philosophical position without proffering a specific set of naturalistic circumstances to which we should reduce the explanation of theistic experiences.

Demons and God

I will give a rationale for the disappearance theory by way of analogy to what happened in scientifically developed cultures to the idea that shamans or divines could perceive evil spirits that were causing a person to be ill, what led, that is, to a 'disappearance theory of demon-perceptions'. Consider a culture where the idea prevails that a variety of demons cause illness, and where shamans or divines supposedly are able to perceive the demons at work when the shamans prepare themselves properly for the occasion following a prescribed ritual.[4] In such a culture, demons play a dual role, one explanatory, and the other perceptual. People invoke demons to explain the presence of illness in a person and affirm demons to be objects of perceptual reports.[5]

Nowadays, most people in Western cultures believe neither that evil spirits cause illness nor that divines really perceive them. Most Westerners have a different explanation of sickness and disease. They know about microbes, antibodies, and so on, and have developed medicines and treatments that cure many ailments and arrest the progress of others. Based on available scientific theories, Western science may not be able to predict just when a particular person will contract a specific illness. Yet, it can do quite a bit of successful predicting, and in many cases when an illness strikes, it knows what will happen in the organism and how to go about dealing with the illness. In addition, the scientific story gives us an idea of the mechanisms involved in the contracting of illnesses, providing ways to prevent outbreaks of sickness and plagues. The idea that spirits cause illness provides no such benefits. So scientifically influenced cultures have replaced the demon-explanation of illness with a scientific story with powerful theoretical (and practical) advantages over the demon story.

Now, as long as the demon-explanation was in force, when shamans or divines *seemed* to see demons near a sick person, there was good reason to think they really did see them, those very demons who, by common belief, were causing the malady. After all, the demons were in the vicinity. However, after the abandonment of the demon explanation, it was no longer compelling to think divines enjoyed reliable demon-perceptions. It became preferable to think shamans were hallucinating, that what they actually saw were demon-hallucinations and not real demons. There existed no need for demons in order to explain disease. Therefore, we looked for what we knew about self-induced trances and substances ingested in order to 'see' demons, hoping to find some alternative explanation there. In the absence of support for the demon-hypothesis as explanatory of illness, we were freed up to turn

to possible alternative explanations for shamans seeming to see demons. We
had good reason to prefer the hypothesis that divines were having demon
hallucinations to saying they were really seeing demons. Demons disap-
peared from our explanations.

One version of the disappearance theory would simply remove demons
from the explanation of disease and perceptions of shamans. It would not
bother to deny the existence of demons. A person might embrace this
version and yet continue believing in the existence of demons, perhaps on
'faith'. Another version would deny the existence of demons altogether,
declaring that 'we are not in need of that hypothesis'.

Analogously, a disappearance theory of God-perceptions would start by
noting how God's special actions used to be invoked to explain a splendid
array of natural events. For example, when a child would become ill with
fever, the parent might interpret this as an act of God, and pray to God to
rescind the evil decree. Nowadays that same parent, even if of a religious
mind, likely will attribute the fever to the child's exposure to microbes. The
parent will see the fever as a nuisance, requiring a visit to the doctor, and the
giving of medicine daily for a number of days. When these steps are taken,
the nuisance will usually pass. In this way, scientific explanations have been
steadily replacing theistic explanations of specific events.

As long as God was conceived of as acting here and now in special acts
that intruded upon the natural world, that supported thinking God might be
experienced while so acting. So when the Children of Israel thought God
was splitting the sea for them, they could think they saw God's 'mighty arm'
on the sea, then and there. A parent with a child with a dangerous disease,
believing God was presently acting to help the child get well, might believe
God's active presence could be felt at the child's bedside. The assumed
circumstance of special providential activity created the occasion for supposing God really was perceived.

In addition, as long as people invoked God's special actions for explaining other events in the world, miraculous events, there would have been
support for invoking God's special activity as well in God appearing to a
person in a mystical experience. The background of supernatural intervening action in the world supported thinking God also could be acting in a
special way to initiate a mystical experience of God.

The more we have replaced God's special providence with scientific
explanations, the more we have lost the basis for thinking God was experientially available in conjunction with specific events at a certain place and
time. The context, remember, underwrote the shaman's perception of the
demons – the demons were detected near where they were assumed to be
causing sickness. Claim to see the demons far from where sickness visits,
and your claim would be weakened accordingly. Once God's specific causal
activity recedes, accordingly we lose a basis for explaining why God has
been perceived here and now. In addition, the steep decline in God's special
miraculous activity in the world in general, decreases the attraction of

thinking God would act in a special way to become revealed to someone in a mystical experience. We should now find it more attractive to believe some scientific explanation will explain it all. Relieved of the pressure of theistic explanations of particular events, now we are free to turn to other factors for alternative explanations of theistic experiences.

A drawback to this approach is that the cases of the demons and God are importantly different, however. God is conceived of as creator and sustainer of the universe. God, if existing, is active at every moment and every place in creation. Therefore, as Aquinas has argued, God is present everywhere. Hence, one could argue that when we assess God-perceptions, we address a situation quite different from the demon case. God is causally active every-where, and perceptually available anywhere, if not by special providence then by general providence. When it comes to assessing alleged God-experiences, therefore, we cannot assume that, because special providence has been weakened, if it indeed has, therefore God is not 'available' perceptu-ally. The disappearance theory of God-perceptions will require supplemen-tation by insisting on a scientific explanation for the existence of the world replacing God's creative and sustaining power. Consequently, a disappear-ance theorist might want to eliminate God altogether on the grounds that 'we have no use for that hypothesis' in any sphere of explanation.

Bagger's Conventionalist Argument

Matthew Bagger has boldly defended a version of the 'disappearance theory', with a well-developed argument that God-perceptions cannot constitute evi-dence for people having genuinely perceived God (Bagger, 1999). Bagger's argument depends on a 'conventionalist' understanding of 'justification'. I turn to an examination of Bagger's argument.

Bagger argues that the theistic explanation of mystical experiences of God, that God is genuinely perceived, 'requires a commitment to supernatu-ral causation' (p. 198). However, according to him, supernatural causation is not an acceptable sort of explanation. Therefore, we must reject the theistic explanation of mystical experiences of God. Let us look at this reasoning more closely.

Bagger argues that: 'The modern ideal of a unified sphere of inquiry with no areas immune from naturalistic explanation renders supernatural expla-nation suspect and in need of defense' (p. 198). Bagger proceeds to detail this assertion. He cites the 'centrality of institutions of inquiry' being 'com-pletely independent of religious commitment' as a particularly crucial fea-ture of 'modern life' (p. 218). Thus, the modern inquirer 'rejects any presupposition to inquiry not based on the natural evidence available to him and assumes everything ultimately explicable in terms of a unified casual structure' (p. 218). Not only does modern inquiry not invoke the supernatu-ral to explain the natural, 'the supernatural itself becomes a subject of naturalistic explanations' (p. 219).

As a result, claims Bagger, in modern inquiry (p. 221):

> we never reach the point where we declare a naturalistic explanation of discrete
> events occurring within the natural order unattainable in principle. The success
> of modern modes of inquiry reinforces this tendency. The incredibly rapid pace
> of knowledge growth over the last several centuries confirms a hesitation to
> declare some phenomenon in principle inexplicable on natural principles.

Bagger compares the invocation of God to explain mystical experiences
to the invocation of miracles to explain natural phenomena. Just as 'the
intransigence of certain well-attested anomalies no longer leads to supernatural explanations, but rather to future insight into natural processes' (p.
223), so even if we lack a ready alternative explanation for God-perceptions,
we should not settle for a supernatural explanation. Indeed 'The mere pro-
tracted inability to explain something naturalistically could never in itself
legitimate a supernatural explanation' (p. 227). The elimination of miracles
from our explanatory vocabulary should be matched by an elimination of a
supernatural explanation of mystical experiences of God.

Bagger concludes by advising that 'Theism's cultural relevance relies on
the fact that it does not detract from the modern ideal of epistemic flourishing.' Theism, therefore, should not present itself in 'reactionary and unacceptable forms' (p. 227). Invoking supernatural explanation presents theism
in such a reactionary light. Some theologians have concurred with this
advice to theism. The theologian John MacQuarrie argues for a non-
interventionist theism in the name of a scientific conception of explanation
much as Bagger does (MacQuarrie, 1977, pp. 247–8):

> The traditional conception of miracle is irreconcilable with our modern under-
> standing of both science and history. Science proceeds on the assumption that
> whatever events occur in the world can be accounted for in terms of other events
> that also belong within the world; and if on some occasions we are unable to
> give a complete account of some happening – and presumably all our accounts
> fall short of completeness – the scientific conviction is that further research will
> bring to light further factors in the situation, but factors that will turn out to be
> just as immanent and this-worldly as those already known.

MacQuarrie's constraint on miracles applies to mystical experiences of God
as well.

If Bagger is right, here we have an in-principle objection to supposing
that anyone ever has a genuine perception of God. So, if Bagger is right, we
do not need a live alternative explanation to the theistic explanation of
mystical experiences of God in order to resist the latter. We should resist the
latter in the name of our epistemic standards. Therefore, God disappears
from our explanation of mystical experiences of God.

Bagger rejects a defense he attributes to William Alston (1991). On this
defense, taking perceptions of God as evidentially worthy does not require

invoking the supernatural as an 'explanation' of the perceptions. Instead, claiming direct perception of God, one is prima-facie justified in relying straightaway on one's perceptual experiences. Alston presents an alternative 'perceptual construal' to the 'explanatory construal' of the justification of mystical experiences of God. Alston writes that on the 'explanatory construal', which he rejects (p. 66), 'The subject must have sufficient *reasons* for this supposition if it is to be justified, whereas on the perceptual construal there is at least the possibility of a direct knowledge of God, not based on reasons …', and that on the explanatory construal (pp. 66–7):

> the subject is faced with the task of justifying a causal hypothesis before he can warrantedly claim to be perceiving God; whereas if the experience is given a perceptual construal from the start, we will at least have to take seriously the view that a claim to be perceiving God is prima facie acceptable on its own merits.

Alston wishes to contend that a direct perception of God can justify relying on it on the very grounds that it is a *perception* of God, and not because we invoke God in an *explanation* for why a person has an experience of a certain type. In that way, we detour around the issue about what kinds of 'explanations' are legitimate, relying on the presumed reliability, everything else being equal, of perceptual episodes.

Bagger's response to Alston consists in invoking a conception of experience on which 'experience is explanation' (p. 200). As Bagger puts it, 'In the very making of a perceptual claim, one implicitly commits to the belief that the situation is best explained by the presence of the object allegedly perceived' (p. 200). Bagger continues: 'Even more to the point, the mystical perceiver in particular must have a commitment to the belief that God can and does appear to him in the midst of the natural world' (pp. 200–201). Hence, in any case, the mystical perceiver will have to invoke God's activity when explaining the mystical episode, whether perceptual or not. 'Perception', as Bagger puts it, 'entails explanatory commitments' (p. 201).

In order to reply effectively to Alston, Bagger need not go so far as to assert that, in making a perceptual claim, one implicitly believes that the situation is 'best explained' by the presence of the object allegedly perceived. It is enough to point out, as he does, that were we to inquire about the explanation of how one perceived God, the theistic explanation would utilize supernatural explanation. If supernatural explanation were a problem, as Bagger says, this would reflect back upon perceptions of God as no less problematic.

The thesis that a perceptual claim always involves an implicit judgment about a best explanation seems doubtful, in any case. Children, for example, who do not yet have the concept of a 'best explanation', or cannot yet work with it, are able to make perceptual claims in confidence. There seems to be a built-in mechanism of taking apparent objects of perception as real objects of perception, until counter-reasons arise. Moreover, these judgments seem to be based on the immediacy of perception. Bagger may be correct about a certain class of perceptual judgments, but probably not correct about most of them.

Nonetheless, Bagger is correct about our having to utilize supernatural explanation when we come to the stage of explaining God-perceptions. So, if supernatural explanation falls, so will genuine perceptions of God. On Bagger's view, then, God 'disappears' from the explanation of God-perceptions even before the discovery of a specified set of naturalistic circumstances affording an alternative explanation of those perceptions.

Bagger presents his commitment to 'modern' modes of inquiry and explanation as following from his conventionalist approach to 'justification' and 'good explanation'. 'To justify a belief', writes Bagger, 'one must offer good explanatory reasons, reasons that, when viewed against the background of all one does not currently doubt, contribute to the best overall explanatory account of the phenomena in question' (1999, p. 83). Concepts of justification, therefore, vary for Bagger with conceptions of what are 'good explanations'.[6] Bagger writes that, 'We cannot enumerate any formal criteria of justified belief ... Any candidate for justification must conform to an ideal of human epistemic flourishing. Ideals of human flourishing, however, bear the distinctive marks of time and place, era and culture' (p. 86). We cannot enumerate any formal account of 'good explanation' either. In Bagger's view, 'To construct timeless canons of explanatory goodness for universal application overlooks both the pragmatic element (interest-relativity) in explanation and the historical and cultural relativity of epistemic values' (p. 86).[7] What constitutes justification and a good reason is thus a matter of convention.

Bagger does not conclude that necessarily each culture or period is isolated epistemically from every other, but holds out the possibility, at least, of cultures sharing enough epistemic assumptions for cross-evaluation. Nonetheless, 'the justificatory status of a belief can vary from culture to culture, and from one historical epoch to another' (p. 87). Just so, goodness of explanation can vary from culture to culture, and from one historical epoch to another.

The point of Bagger making his argument a matter of the conventional meaning of 'explanation' is that he does not have to argue for the superiority of the current concept of explanation to which he appeals. To turn back alternative explanatory models it is sufficient to be able to show that they depart from the prevailing convention concerning what is a good explanation. It as though Bagger renders supernatural explanation not just wrong, but incoherent within the cultural-intellectual atmosphere in which it is raised. It is an alleged conceptual, not empirical, mistake to appeal to supernatural explanation in Bagger's culture in this day and age.

This conventionalist conception of good explanation, then, determines Bagger's endorsement of 'modern' modes of inquiry that preclude supernatural explanation. He shows how Teresa of Avila could have been justified in her time and cultural setting in placing a supernatural explanation on her mystical experiences. Her concept of good explanation allowed such an interpretation of her mystical episodes. We today in a scientific culture, however, are precluded from invoking supernatural explanation. The latter do not fit our present concept of justification and good explanation. Bagger appeals to this conventionalist thesis for the sake of what I have called the 'disappearance theory of mystical experiences of God'.

Reply to Bagger   When Bagger contends that we cannot enumerate 'formal criteria' for justification and good explanation, if he means we find no explicitly formulated criteria 'timelessly' across cultures, he is no doubt correct. However, it would be a mistake to conclude from this that there are no conceptions of good explanation implicitly at work across various cultures and periods. Diversity can be a function of differing conceptions of good explanation, but also of starting from different justified beliefs, of different talents in applying criteria of good explanation, and of differing powers of imagination in framing ideas and testing them out. Perhaps the best theory about good explanation will turn out to be that there are some, at least, implicit rules to be found just about wherever we look. Thus, two different styles of thinking may be subsumable under a general conception of good explanation, with the differences accountable for otherwise. The issues here are large and difficult. They include issues such as to what degree our concepts prescind from their practical application to reach a high level of abstraction and to what degree our concepts are immanent in our working paradigms. If we think of a specific concept of good explanation depending strongly on specific moves paradigmatic of explanation on the ground, as Bagger does, we will be less prepared to recognize (some, at least) implicit standards of explanation than otherwise. In any case, the conventionalist conception of explanation, and justification, remains controversial in philosophy and by no means has won the day.[8] Nevertheless, in what follows I will grant Bagger his conventionalist position.[9]

One wonders where Bagger gets his information about the cultural dominance of scientific explanation to the exclusion of supernatural explanation. I wonder to what extent people do hold to a 'modern ideal' of explanation, excluding the supernatural. Moreover, I wonder who are the 'we' in his statement that 'we never reach the point where we declare a naturalistic explanation of discrete events occurring within the natural order unattainable in principle'. My wonder arises because Bagger ignores the massive numbers of traditional religious believers in modern societies like the United States, in which he writes. For tens of millions of religious devotees supernatural explanation is alive and well. Bagger also ignores a mass culture that sociologists have documented as a new religious paradigm in Western countries, most especially the United States. This is the movement of 'new spirituality' that appeals to inner experience and devotion, yet is unconnected to traditional organized religion. The sociologist Phillip Wexler has written of this phenomenon as an emerging 'mystical society' with a new social vision (Wexler, 2000). 'The new society is mystical', writes Wexler, 'because it is about the quest for direct experience of the transcendental', invites an 'immediacy' that is the 'hallmark of a mystical consciousness and life' (p. 15). Here too supernatural explanation lives and thrives.

Here is how the sociologist, Robert Wuthnow, who has studied the new spirituality, describes the situation in the United States at the end of the twentieth century (Wunthow, 1998, p.1, quoted in Wexler, 2000, p. 117):

> Judging from newspapers and television, American's fascination with spiritual-ity has been escalating dramatically. Millions of people report miraculous inter-ventions in their lives by such forces as guardian angels who help them avoid danger and spirit guides who comfort them in moments of despair. Faced with death, many people report seeing a brilliant tunnel of light that embraces them in its mysterious glory – and live to write best selling books about these experi-ences. When pollsters ask, Americans overwhelmingly affirm their faith in God, claiming to pray often to that God.

There is no denying, therefore, a prominent, pervasive cultural phenomenon of happily using supernatural explanation along with recognition of scien-tific modes of inquiry. Whether the two go well together is beside the point when trying to ascertain the conventionally recognized types of good expla-nation out there in the world. Out there in the world, it is far from true that scientific inquiry has supplanted supernatural explanation. So in empirical terms alone Bagger's case seems weak.

Bagger, of course, is right that many people in his Western culture, principally secularists, do exclude supernatural explanation in the name of modern modes of inquiry. Apparently two subcultures live together in mod-ern societies, one that thinks in terms of supernatural explanation and one that does not. The naysay subculture might be more prominent than the former in the sense of having greater access to political centers of power in Western states. Yet it is hard to say which one reflects, in numbers and cultural significance, a dominant convention concerning 'good explanation' in modern Western societies.

Suppose Bagger somehow were able to show empirically the domi-nance of an exclusively scientific understanding of what makes for a good explanation. Perhaps the religious and spiritual cultures signify no more than an 'under-culture' to the culture guided exclusively by scientific modes of inquiry (though I strongly doubt this). Even then, I would find unacceptable Bagger's rejection of supernatural explanation in the name of a conventionalist defense of contemporary modes of inquiry. Here is why. On Bagger's conventionalist position, shifts in 'good explanation' are not based on epistemic criteria, but are more like *zeitgeist* swings. We should suppose that new explanatory paradigms catch people's interest and set off a shift that carries a culture to a different way of thinking.

Alternatively, we are to suppose that changing values push forward new or dormant ways of explaining. Of course, such changes do not take place overnight.

Philosophers of knowledge have described the complex processes involved in scientific paradigm shifts (see Kuhn, 1962; Lakatos, 1978a and 1978b). Scientific paradigms arise, may lie dormant, compete between themselves, become dominant, wane, and sometimes return. Proposals are made. Some catch on, while others are dropped. Some linger until found attractive later on. Others burst into sight and fade quickly. In addition, dropped paradigms can stay around in a subdued voice alongside newly dominant ideas. There is every reason to believe that shifts of paradigms in explanation would be as fluid and dynamic, and surely as complex and winding, as are scientific paradigm-shifts.

Since this is so, I find unacceptable an a priori rejection of supernatural explanation because of contemporary modes of inquiry. Nothing in the conventionalist story could possibly generate an a priori prohibition purely in the name of a dominant current fashion in explanation. To invoke dominant current vogues of good explanation as a roadblock to the advancing of alternatives contradicts the natural way in which ideas of good explanation arise, challenge and flourish. To reject alternatives solely because they are not the dominant mode of explanation would be to wield conventionalism unjustly as a protective strategy of a most conservative kind. If this is what Bagger is up to, I find an inner inconsistency, if not incoherence, in Bagger's conventionalist argument against supernatural explanation.

Bagger does look for support from the 'success' of modern modes of inquiry and to the 'rapid growth of knowledge' afforded therein, as a reason for going modern and scorning supernatural explanation. By Bagger's conventionalist lights, however, that talk can reflect only the epistemic standards of 'modern' modes of inquiry themselves and does not support those modes from the 'outside' as it were. 'Success' and 'knowledge' do not have formal criteria, on conventionalism, any more than do justification and good explanation. Therefore, Bagger cannot invoke them in favor of modern modes of inquiry as a way of stifling possible alternative sources of good explanation. They themselves only reflect once again the dominant conception of what makes for good explanation.

Instead of vetoing it the way he does, Bagger might have addressed supernatural explanation directly by considering its potential or lack of it for 'epistemic flourishing'. For example, he might have discussed theistic philosophers who have labored to square divine activity with a modern scientific understanding of the world.[10] For these philosophers, and those like them, supernatural explanation belongs in the category of 'good explanation' along with Bagger's scientific, naturalistic explanations. One way to argue against supernatural explanation would have been to show that these theistic attempts failed, or must fail. This Bagger does not attempt to do. Bagger fails to give persuasive reason why a person for whom God's activity in the world is a live option should ignore the theistic understanding of mystical experiences of God.

What, though, of people for whom supernatural explanation is not a live option, those who think of good explanation exclusively as scientific explanation? These will include both Baggerian conventionalists as well as defenders of the analogy to demon-perceptions. How should they evaluate the Argument from Perception? For them, the idea that mystical experiences of God are genuine, implying supernatural explanation, would be a proposal to shift their thinking and admit supernatural explanation as a category of explanation. In all likelihood, therefore, for a person for whom God's activity in the world is not a live option, the Argument from Perception will fail to persuade. If it is going to be persuasive for these people the defender of the argument will have to place it within a larger, supplementing context, granting respectability to supernatural explanation. I now want to outline how a defender of the Argument from Perception might try to supplement the argument to make the supernatural explanation required for genuine experiences of God a live option for a good explanation.

Firstly, the defender of the Argument from Perception might point out that contemporary canons of explanation were formed not so much in full awareness of the rich historical phenomenon of mystical experiences of God, but rather by choosing to ignore it entirely. Hence, the current, non-theistic models of good explanation were born in sin, ignoring what many have and continue to consider a good explanation for these experiences, namely a supernatural explanation. Why should this mode of explanation be unacceptable? One reason would be fear of having then to relate seriously to traditional religion, or fear of being asked to buy into a host of what one takes to be superstitious beliefs lurking about traditional forms of religion. This would be a form of the Next Thing You Known Syndrome that I have argued earlier we should disclaim in our discussion. Another reason, alluded to just above, would be fear that the success of science would thereby be impeded, a clamoring for supernatural explanation competing with sober naturalistic ones. This is a very important point, and the defender of the Argument from Perception will want to provide a reasonable defense of supernatural explanation not hurting the advance of science. As I have already noted, Bagger does nothing to show this direction cannot be successful.

Secondly, a defender of the Argument from Perception might be willing to offer a non-interventionist conception of genuine God-perceptions. That is, a defender might be willing to contend that genuine mystical experiences of God could be explained by non-interventionist supernatural activity. The explanation of genuine God-perceptions would be in terms of how God created and designed the world, a world that thereafter afforded experiences of God in accordance with its stable, ongoing laws and structures, and in accordance with God's purposes and intentions. Perhaps, as William Alston has suggested, God is always experientially available, our needing only the proper naturalistic conditions to succeed in perceiving God. A naturalistic explanation of this sort would have to modify the notion that God initiates perceptual encounters with God, an idea implying interventionist metaphysics. God's 'making God available' to us in mystical perception would turn into a metaphor for the elusive and variable naturalistic conditions necessary for perceiving God in a mystical way. In particular, we would need a naturalistic story about how training in non-egocentrism was necessary, in most cases, for mystical success. An appropriate theory about brain activity and mystical experience might help matters along here.[11] God's original acts, purposes and intentions would hover above all of that.

This move would rid us only of interventionist supernatural explanation, leaving us with the category of the supernatural nonetheless. However, the move would help ameliorate some of the resistance from worries over the integrity of science.

Thirdly, the defender of the Argument from Perception will want to marshal philosophical arguments against an exclusively naturalistic understanding of the world, forcing recognition in any case of the category of supernatural explanation. One important endeavor in this direction has been Robert Adams' argument that natural science cannot explain the correlation between phenomenal qualia, such as flavors and colors, and physical states that obtain in perceptual experience. Adams argues that a theological explanation is required for this (Adams, 1987). A second important anti-naturalist argument is due to Alvin Plantinga. Plantinga contends against the idea that human knowledge could have come about from evolutionary development in a naturalistic way. The most we could expect from evolution is that we would have beliefs adaptive for survival. However, adaptive beliefs need not be true, and Plantinga argues that on purely naturalistic assumptions we should not expect them to be true. Thus, we should maintain that God guides the evolutionary process to bring about not only adaptive but also true, reliable beliefs about the world (Plantinga, 1993). And of course, another way of trying to dispute naturalism would be to argue that it could not account for the existence of the universe, *per se.*

When all is said and done, however, the Argument from Perception, even with full supplementation, might not convince a person for whom supernatural explanation is not a live option. This means, in turn, that the Argument from Perception even with supplementing will not be universally rationally compelling, in the sense of justifying its conclusion to all who would ponder its premises carefully. This is an important point, but falls short of Bagger's ambition. It does not show that anyone who considers Bagger's conventionalist argument should reject the Argument from Perception.

To conclude, what we should learn from Bagger is not that we can employ an automatic veto of a theistic explanation of mystical experiences of God. Instead, we should learn that for people for whom a supernatural explanation is otherwise not a live option, the Argument from Perception would probably fail to generate initial evidential sufficiency for the theistic explanation of God-perceptions. For others, the Argument from Perception for initial evidential sufficiency stands.

Notes

1   For an earlier, and somewhat different presentation of the distinction, see Gellman, 1997, Chapter Five.
2   For a criticism of Oakes's argument see Wainwright, 1981.
3   I am indebted here to a conversation with Yakir Levine.
4   I have stolen the term 'disappearance theory' as well as the example, modified, from Rorty, 1965.
5   Robin Horton has analyzed the dual roles of spirits and demons in explanation and what he calls 'communion' in Horton, 1993, especially Chapter One.
6   One could question Bagger's way of linking justification to good explanation. I will not pursue that issue here.
7   According to Bagger, the pragmatic element of justification includes as well that justification has relevance only when justifying oneself to others (Bagger, 1999, Chapter Three).
8   The issues here are entangled with the divide in philosophy between pro-Wittgensteinian and non-Wittgensteinian philosophers. Bagger explicitly lines up with the former.
9   Susan Haack has argued against conventionalism in Haack, 1993, Chapter Nine.
10 For a particularly ingenious attempt with regard to miracles, see Cover, 1999. See also Richard Swinburne, 1989. William Alston, 1986, has argued for divine activity being consistent with the findings of science.
11 See the following chapter where I discuss neuropsychological explanations of mystical experiences of God.

Chapter 5

Alternative Explanations II: Sociological and Neuropsychological Proposals

A thorough study of the array of alternative explanations that people have proposed for mystical experiences of God would require an extensive scientific investigation. That undertaking is beyond the limits of the present study and beyond the powers of the present author. Instead in this chapter I take upon myself a more restricted task. I select for examination three challenging proposals, one sociological and two neuropsychological. I intend the discussion of these three proposals and their deficiencies to clarify the sort of issues that arise in assessing alternative explanations. I hope to contribute to an understanding of what it would take to come up with a successful reductionist alternative to the theistic interpretation of mystical experiences of God.

Fales's Sociological Explanation

Evan Fales has written that, 'the scientific study of mysticism is a long jump ahead of theistic explanations, which not only cannot handle the full body of data in any natural or plausible way, but which have little or nothing to tell us about the mechanisms by means of which God intrudes His presence into human perceptual experience' (Fales, 1996b, p. 313). Accordingly, Fales offers an engaging sociological explanation of the phenomenon of mystical perceptions of God. His theory has the alleged advantages of explaining a greater range of data than the theistic explanation of those same experiences, and of making use of otherwise familiar mechanisms – sociological and secondarily psychological – to explain the phenomenon. Therefore, Fales's approach exemplifies a reductionist strategy of the theoretical type noted in the previous chapter. Fales desires to promote a better explanation than the theistic one of God-perceptions, and to conclude that subjects do not genuinely perceive God. Fales maintains that the sociological explanation, with supplementation, not only removes the grounds for taking mystical experiences to be veridical, but also, by providing a better explanation, gives adequate grounds for denying that mystical experiences are veridical. 'Tacking on' a theistic cause to the sociological story, says Fales, is 'ad hoc and awkward', and so should be disallowed. So Fales is a truth-reductionist.[1]

Fales bases his sociological explanation on studies by the anthropologist I.M. Lewis on spirit possession, linking the latter to the securing of social and political power.[2] Fales generalizes from Lewis's findings to contend that the true explanation of theistic mysticism is in the political power and ability for social control it confers on the mystic. Fales says, 'mysticism serves as a means of access to political and social power or control' and that 'the employment of mystical strategies ... to gain these ends ... display fairly clear patterns' (Fales, 1996a, p. 149). Fales's sociological explanation of mystical experiences of God possesses an initial attractiveness since it shares our new-found awareness of how the dynamics of power, social control and domination can drive seemingly 'innocent' human phenomena. By assimilating our understanding of mystical experience to more general structures of explanation, Fales hopes to gain a strong theoretical edge over the theistic explanation.

The story starts with Lewis's theory about 'spirit possession'. Spirit possession involves a spirit (or spirits) entering into and taking control of a person's body and mind. When so 'possessed', people act in bizarre, ostensibly uncontrollable ways until the spirit is exorcised. While possessed, subjects' acts are thought to be those of the possessing spirit and not of the subjects themselves.

Lewis studied spirit possession in various cultures, and distinguished between politically and socially *peripheral* and *central* possession cults. In cults that are peripheral in the social structure, spirit possession allows marginalized individuals a measure of power not otherwise available to them. The possessing spirit is alien to the central cult and ominous in character, so others must mollify it, entailing special treatment for the person possessed. Lewis's examples include tribes where women are marginalized in the power structure, especially in relation to their husbands. In these tribes, diverse peripheral cults of possession have developed, mainly composed of women, in which a woman possessed by a spirit is allowed unusual behavior for a woman and/or in which the possessing spirit must be placated by the woman receiving lavish presents from her husband. Women so possessed form groups dedicated to the cult spirit, perpetuating the practice. Lewis theorizes that the cult serves the purpose of obtaining gains not available to the possessed 'victim' in the controlling power relations. The cults thrive where open resistance is not possible, but sometimes develop in time into straightforward rebellion.

Lewis cites an illuminating example of how peripheral cults function in this way from Elizabeth Colson's study of the Tonga of Zambia (Colson, 1969). Among the plateau Tonga, the traditional pattern of relations between men and women displays relative gender equality. Women participate in Tonga social life as do men and are not subject to constraints imposed by men. Accordingly, Colson found that the peripheral cult of *masabe* spirit-possession was rare.

The valley Tonga, on the other hand, live in a different social structure. Women remain home while men participate in the 'outside world'. Women remain secluded, and *masabe* spirits periodically possess them. Possession takes the form of spirits demanding to be placated by gifts from husbands, otherwise not available to these excluded women, including luxury goods and soap. 'Thus,' writes Lewis, 'contrasting the record of these cults among the valley Tonga with possession on the plateau, it is clear how in the former case much of the traditional inequality between the sexes continues and so the cults continue ... For the plateau Tonga, with their more liberal treatment of women, such possession of this type as exists continues to affect men and women equally' (Lewis, 1986, pp. 41–2).

In central possession cults, the cult is part of the central establishment and the possessing spirits are recognized by the dominant cult. Here too possession serves for access to power, but this time by non-marginalized persons, typically men, who aspire to central power where there is no defined route to obtaining it. Spirit possession confers an uncommon status on the possessed, gaining them access to the centers of power. Thus, Lewis finds that in tribes that determine power ascriptively, for example when power passes from father to son, central possession cults do not prosper. Then spirit possession is just not a way to get power. In addition, in societies that pass from fluidity to rigidity in power ascription, central possession wanes. Spirit possession no longer serves as a path to power and influence.

Lewis observes that in both peripheral and central cults there exists a rhetoric of the 'involuntary' nature of spirit possession, including affliction at the onset of possession. The subject alleges to resist the possession and to seek relief and release. The supposed involuntary character of possession, infers Lewis, serves to mask the individual's desire for power, and creates the supposed need to placate the spirit with gifts and obedience, not the 'victim'. Hence, the great power potential for the subject concealed in mystical possession.

This is a sketchy summary of Lewis's rich and instructive study of possession cults, but will do for our purposes. Missing is an adequate account of psychological mechanisms by which the desire for power or control give rise to the claim to be possessed. Lewis attempts to provide a psychoanalytic account of this (Lewis, 1986, Chapter Seven), but Fales raises his own possibilities here. These include self-deception by the subject and a psychological propensity on the part of some to have possession-like experiences in the tense circumstances of social or political privation. Fales includes as well the suggestion of implicit agreement wherein all concerned understand spirit possession to be a fiction and go along with it for its redeeming social value. Spirit possession serves as a safety valve in releasing unexpressed social pressures.

Fales proposes generalizing Lewis's sociological explanation from Lewis's findings for tribal possession cults to theistic mystical experiences. Theistic mystical experience serves for the gaining of power and social influence. The power sought would not normally be for the mystics' own glorification, but for the benefit of marginalized groups with which they identified.

Fales presents Teresa of Avila as a paradigm case of Lewis's theory, applied to theistic experience. Based on updated studies, Fales depicts Teresa as triply marginalized in her social-political reality: as a woman, unmarried, and a member of a Jewish *converso* family in Spain after the expulsion of the Jews. We discover with Teresa, as in spirit possession, the rhetoric of the involuntary nature of her experiences and of her affliction. Teresa's mystical guise, so Fales contends, is what afforded her access to power in the Church as well as an advantage for criticizing contemporary society and the Church. Fales writes that (1996a, p. 146):

> Teresa's experiences have left her, she claims, with certain insights into human affairs. Her understanding of what is valued in heaven enables her, in fact, to launch a strikingly bold attack upon certain of the human values and social conventions of her time. The attack is most persistently directed against the contemporary conception of personal and familiar honour ...

Without her aura of mysticism she would have remained powerless. Fales notes (p. 146):

> That Teresa's critique of society comes out of her ecstatic experiences is no accident. It is precisely because those experiences are so fraught with pain and difficulty that they provide Teresa, a woman with no other source of authority, with a moral platform from which such criticisms can be effectively launched.

So Teresa's mysticism is well explained by her extensive social marginalization and consequent desire for power.

Teresa does not quite fit Lewis's typology, since her 'possessing spirit', God or Jesus, belongs to the 'central cult' of her Christian milieu. This should not have been the chosen route for a marginalized person such as Teresa. Fales explains this deviation quite nicely in terms of the dangers in Teresa's time, for women in particular, of being accused of witchcraft or demon possession. This danger precluded the wise from claiming propensity toward peripheral mystic experiences. Hence, Teresa goes the route of the central cult, which in this case provides access into centers of power.

The single confirming instance of Teresa hardly suffices to establish Fales's sociological thesis for theistic mystics in general. In addition, Fales acknowledges that 'it can hardly be claimed that we have at present conclusive evidence for Lewis's theory (or any other naturalistic account of mystical experience)'(Fales, 1996b, p. 311). Fales predicts (or retrodicts), however, that Lewis's theory will fit well the lives of the great preponderance of theistic mystics.

Fales proceeds to argue that his sociological explanation surpasses the explanatory power of the theistic explanation of perceptions of God (pp. 306–7. His sociological explanation explains well the connection between mysticism and social context for all forms of mysticism, theistic and non-theistic alike. The theistic explanation, conversely, cannot account for the connection for non-theistic mysticism, argues Fales, and is superfluous for theistic experiences. The theistic explanation requires supplementation by further theories, such as Lewis's, for non-theistic mystical phenomena. One theory is better than two. The sociological explanation, contends Fales, merits adoption as that one theory. We do not need the theistic explanation here, and so ought not to 'tack it on' to Fales's sociological explanation.

Critique of Fales

Historical Counterexamples   I begin my critique of Fales by describing the lives of four noteworthy mystics, one Christian and three Jewish, for whom Fales's thesis seems not to work. This will not exactly prove Fales wrong, since these mystics just might be exceptions to the rule. Nevertheless, their stories do cast doubt on the putative connection between power access and being an important theistic mystic.

I begin with my Christian example. Jacob Boehme was an impressive Christian mystic.[3] Boehme was born in 1575, and was a shoemaker, who later turned to commerce. In 1600, at the age of 25, he had a transforming mystical experience. Of this experience he wrote, 'I saw and knew the Being of Beings, the Byss and the Abyss, the eternal generation of the Trinity, the origin and decent of this world, and of all creatures through Divine Wisdom ... I saw, too, the essential nature of evil and of good, and how the pregnant mother ... brought them forth' (quoted in Jones, 1914, pp. 159–60). Boehme testified that this episode changed his life. Yet, for two decades he remained unknown as a mystic, save to a small circle. More than ten years after his experience he completed the first exposition of his spiritual insights, growing out of his mystical experiences. Even then, Boehme made little or no effort to publish his writings or to otherwise promote his fame. A small number of manuscripts, though, did circulate unpublished among a small group of admirers. This led to denunciation by a local guardian of the prevailing orthodoxy and to Boehme's agreement to cease writing. It was only years later, in 1618, under increasing pressure of friends to give the world his new understanding that he began to write in earnest. Still none of his manuscripts were published until 1623, when, without asking his permission, an admirer published three of his works.

Because of resistance to his published ideas, Boehme was forced to leave his city, Gorlitz. He died in 1624, but not before appearing at the Court of the elector of Saxony, about which impending occasion he wrote, 'I am invited there to a conference of high people ... Soon the revelation of Jesus Christ shall break forth and destroy the works of the Devil' (quoted in Jones, 1914, p. 167).

Andrew Weeks describes Boehme as engaging in 'self-promoting activities' from around 1620 until his death (Weeks, 1991, pp. 162ff.). However, I question the strength of Weeks's conclusion based on the evidence he collects for it. We must remember that Boehme was openly attacked at various junctures of his life. Hence, what might otherwise appear to be 'self-promoting activities' might better be understood in the context of Boehme's need to defend himself against those who attacked him on religious grounds.[4] Hence, for example, Weeks's pointing to Boehme having written five letters in his defense in 1621, counts little for Boehme's having sought 'self-promotion'.

The strongest basis for Weeks's claim of Boehme's self-promotion is that the latter saw himself standing for a 'New Reformation', and seems to have made a decision, in 1624, to reach out for a wider influence (pp. 209–10). However, Boehme did not expect the New Reformation to come only through him. More importantly, to make Fales's case out for a given mystic it is not sufficient to know that he thought he was part of a new religious movement. We must also have good reason to believe he took steps to promote such a movement for the sake of gaining power and social influence. This, I submit, Weeks does not establish in Boehme's case.

My principal point in connection with Weeks, however, is this: even if Weeks were right that Boehme engaged in self-promoting activities, these would have taken place twenty years and more after Boehme's initial self-transforming mystical experience. This impressive discontinuity between the formative mystical experience and self-promoting activities counts strongly against linking the former to the latter in the way Fales's theory would have us do.

Jacob Boehme's story hardly reads as a biography of a person who sees mysticism as a path to power for a group with which he identified. For many years, Boehme remained quiet about his experiences, and soon enough realized how unorthodox were his teachings based on them. Boehme's teachings and mystical experiences were not of the central cult, but peripheral relative to his social context. It was precisely this that constrained their utilization for power on Boehme's part. Indeed, Boehme's fame came only several decades after his death. For an inordinate amount of time after starting to have mystical experiences, Boehme was a quiet mystic, a good example of a notable Christian mystic who does not fit Fales's theory.

I turn now to three important Jewish mystics who do not fit Fales's theory either.

For a period of about 150 years, with some small interruption, the descendants of Moses Maimonides (1135–1204) held the position of *nagid,* or head, of the Jewish Community of Egypt. These included Abraham the son of Maimonides (1186–1237); David son of Abraham (1222–1300); Abraham (the Second) son of David (1245–1313); Joshua son of Abraham (the Second) (1310–1355); and David (the Second) son of Joshua (1355–1415).[5] Beginning with Abraham son of Maimonides the position of *nagid* was hereditary, passing from father to son.[6] Of those who held the *nagid* office, two in particular were seriously devoted, practicing Jewish-Sufi mystics: Abraham son of Maimonides, and David son of Joshua.[7] Abraham's *Highways of Perfection* is strongly informed by Sufi mysticism, and David son of

Joshua wrote a work entitled, '*Instructor of Asceticism and Guide to Simplicity*', also a highly mystical Sufi tract (David son of Joshua son of Abraham Maimonides, 1987).

Abraham taught that the aim of a person was the soul's communion with God, and regarded the Sufi practices as the true way to this communion. He declared the Sufi teachings to have been the true, lost teachings of Israel's prophets. In these matters, he parted company with his illustrious father, Maimonides. Of relevance to us is the fact that Abraham ascended to the office of *nagid* at the young age of eighteen (in 1204) due to the fame of his father, Maimonides. Abraham's mysticism played no role here. By the nature of the office, Abraham's personal authority as *nagid* rested on his being an expert in Jewish law, rather than on his mystical activities. His Sufism was not reflective of the central cult, in the Jewish community, and was quite a novelty in the Jewish community. His Sufi-motivated innovations in the synagogue's prayers (such as washing of the feet and falling on the knees during prayer) met with strong opposition from parts of the Egyptian Jewish community (see Goiten, 1988, pp. 491ff.). His Sufi mysticism was decidedly not a source of power and increased authority. Neither did Abraham seek to excommunicate opponents of his Sufi-inspired decrees, although he had the power to do so. If we prefer to see Egyptian Jewry as peripheral in Egyptian society, relative to Islam, we might think of Abraham's Sufism as drawing him closer to the central Islamic cult. However, Sufism was itself peripheral in Islam, and there is no evidence that Abraham sought, or that this brought him, increased power in the larger Egyptian society.

So Abraham son of Maimonides was a mystic for whom there is every reason to believe that mysticism was not designed to provide gains in power and influence, and whose actual power derived from sources other than his mysticism. This profile does not fit Fales's typology.

For a long time, researchers thought that Israel Baal Shem Tov (c.1700–1760) founded a new Jewish movement, Hasidism, in his lifetime. If so, we would expect to find Baal Shem Tov enjoying prerogatives of authority and influence either for himself or for his group. However, new research toward the end of the twentieth century has shown that Hasidism did not conceive itself as a social movement, let alone a mass movement, until after Baal Shem Tov's death. Baal Shem Tov seems to have thought of himself neither as a social leader nor as a wielder of political power. We now have a different picture of this man's life and doings.[8]

The new portrait of Baal Shem Tov is this. In Baal Shem Tov's time there was a recognized vocation amongst the Jewish communities of Eastern Europe of 'practical kabbalism'. Persons of impressive piety who knew secret formulae and magical cures attended to this vocation, and traveled from place to place offering their services or stayed put and had supplicants travel to them. They did not have to have special mystical talents, in the sense of 'mysticism' of this study. They often bore the title, 'Baal Shem' (literally: 'Possessor of a Name') or 'Baal Shem Tov' (literally: 'Possessor of a Good Name'). Israel 'Baal Shem Tov' was one of them. In this capacity he was exempt from paying taxes on his residence in the town of Miedzyboz, where he spent most of his life. Israel Baal Shem Tov was also a great mystic who had experiences of supernal worlds and of God's heavenly court. His mystical talents went well beyond what he needed for his job description in the profession of a 'Baal Shem'.

In the Eastern Europe of Baal Shem Tov, there already existed small, local, loosely organized groups of holy associations of people known as 'Hasidim'. These assemblages dedicated themselves intensely to the study of Jewish mystical texts and practices, in addition to traditional Jewish studies. The small circle of Baal Shem Tov's 'Hasidim' was one of these groups. Baal Shem Tov continued the extant traditions of these Hasidic groups with two innovations. One was that penitence and holiness were not to be bought at the price of asceticism, a position going against the prevailing wisdom. While not being entirely against ascetic practices, Baal Shem Tov did downplay their importance and warned against both the pride and the sadness they engendered. He was in favor of cleaving to God in joy. The second innovation was that mystical prayer did not require knowing the intricate kabbalistic meanings of the words of the prayers. Rather, it depended on concentration upon the letters of the prayers, and on concentrating upon unifying the letters together into words and sentences.[9]

These innovations opened up mystical practices to a potentially larger group than did the previous emphasis on austere asceticism and the need for extensive knowledge of intricate kabbalistic systems in prayer. However, we now know that Baal Shem Tov did not try to found a mass movement and that in his lifetime people did not regard him as an innovator of a new movement. Moshe Rosman, a leader in the new research on Baal Shem Tov, writes (1996, p. 184), 'It is highly doubtful that the Besht [Baal Shem Tov] was aware of the potential effects of these innovations. He directed them at the mystical-ascetic hasidim to improve their chances for Divine communion, and never advocated the expansion of this group... '. Israel Baal Shem Tov died in Miedzyboz as he had lived, with the following of but a limited group of people who sought him out and found him inspiring. The sense of Hasidism as a movement did not solidify until 1772, twelve years after Baal Shem Tov's death, when a proclamation against Hasidism was issued in Vilnus. Hasidism did not become a mass movement until later still.

So the evidence shows that Baal Shem Tov was a prominent Jewish mystic who sought no meaningful power based on his mystical talents, and who did not determine to effect social or political change. He was simply a charismatic to whom some were attracted. Baal Shem Tov hardly fits Fales's mold.

My third Jewish mystic is Rabbi Abraham Isaac Kook (1865–1935), an erudite Talmudic scholar who served as Rabbi in Poland and afterward in Palestine under Turkish rule, and thereafter under the British Mandate.[10] The Jewish masses loved him for his forceful personality, loving temperament, and support for Jewish settlement in Palestine. Under the British, he became Chief Rabbi of Palestine, in which capacity he decided thousands of matters of Jewish law, and wrote legal works and theological tracts. He was also the greatest known Jewish mystic of the twentieth century. He wrote extensively of his mystical life in prose and penned mystical poetry reflecting his inner life.[11]

R. Kook's mystical side had little to do with his obtaining and retaining his various positions of power, as Rabbi or Chief Rabbi. His mystical writings, more in the nature of diaries, were little known and hardly published during his lifetime. The writings published and well known while he was alive were collections of decisions in Jewish law, pamphlets and newspaper articles on current affairs, and philosophical essays. To this day, much of his mystical writing remains in manuscript, waiting for publication.

During his lifetime, R. Kook's following was based on his distinguished scholarship and unusually caring nature. He headed a *yeshivah*, a traditional school of rabbinical study, at which he regularly delivered lectures in Talmud and on other works of Jewish law. He also gave lectures on Jewish philosophical and ethical tracts, and wrote a defense of the rationalist philosopher Maimonides. Some of these lectures and some of his writings used mystical kabbalistic sources. These, however, were not the basis of his fame or for his authority.

Rabbi Kook lived in two worlds, the world of the Talmudic, legal expert, and the world of the mystical life. The latter played only a small role, if any, in his attainments of positions of power and authority. He too does not fit Fales's hypothesis.

Finally, I would like to point out that among women mystics, Teresa, Fales's model mystic, seems to stands out as one of the exceptions to what was typically the denial of power to a woman because of her mystical talents. The institution of anchorage that was used in the Middle Ages to shut away women anchoress mystics for years, will attest to this. Feminist scholars of religion have presented the sad story in detail (see Jantzen, 1995 and 1988; and Beer, 1993). Fales's thesis neglects these historical findings.

These brief accounts raise serious doubts about the truth of Fales's thesis that the mysticism of important mystics served them as a means to social and political power. In order to make good his claim, Fales owes us a great number of more illustrations of his thesis.

So far I have been expressing doubts about Fales's thesis from historical counter-examples. In addition, there are several general considerations counting against Fales's sociological explanation. As a philosopher, I am not in a position to judge whether Lewis's work on spirit possession is acceptable, though I know it has some detractors.[12] So I will simply assume it correct for the sake of argument, and concentrate here on reasons for declining to apply the findings for spirit possession to theistic mystical experiences, as does Fales.

Non-institutionalized mysticism   There is a telling difference between spirit possession that occurs within an established, ritualized cult, or a cult in the making, whether central or peripheral, and phenomena that occur independently of extant or evolving organized, institutional structures. In Lewis's peripheral cults, an existing or evolving social institution defines and honors the power prerogatives of the possessed subject (see Lewis, 1986 and 1989). An example is spirit possession among Somali women that requires (and in a sense permits) the husband to ease his wife's anomalous state, by, among other things, buying expensive gifts for her. In central cults, the organized cult provides a path accessible to the non-marginalized mystic on which to move with the hope of gaining power.

The presence of set paths of accessibility to power might make mysticism an inviting, rational option for a subject suffering power deprivation. However, when mystical possession is independent of inviting social institutions, or when the mystic is not well placed for access to power, the mystical route is much less opportune and thus less of a rational option for seeking power. Mystics will then have to gain power, if that's what they want, by dint of their personalities, in ways they must themselves devise. In such circumstances, then, it lacks plausibility to imagine mystics are motivated by a desire for power and social influence, for their group or themselves. The amount of effort and ingenuity they would have to invest in order to gain power, when the power is by no means ensured, counts against this as a rational strategy.

In the long history of theistic mystical experiences, often we are looking at cultures of non-institutionalized theistic mysticism or at times at which being a mystic is not an easy or ready path to fame and authority. We have here, therefore, initial reason to doubt that Fales's position on theistic mysticism is correct for the general picture.

Garden-variety mysticism   It is common knowledge that people who do not fall into the category of 'great' or 'important' mystics have theistic mystical experiences. They are unassuming folk, who go about their everyday lives without becoming known as 'professional' mystics. Neither do they seek or gain a meaningful measure of power thanks to their mystical propensities. Various studies have been made of what we might call 'garden-variety' mysticism.[13] Robert Elwood cites a Gallup poll conducted in the late 1970s finding that 31 per cent of respondents reported having had a religious or mystical experience (Elwood, 1999, p. 2). Of these, one third described their experiences as of a 'divine being'. If even 50 per cent of the respondents were telling the truth, this would be a significant number of 'ordinary' people reporting experiences of a relevant kind. Even were Fales right about the 'great' mystics, his theory would not be sufficient to undermine the evidential value of the theistic experiences of 'ordinary mystics'.

Fales is aware of this response. 'Might there not be more private, personal, and sporadic instances of mystical experience which persist, as it were, below or barely at the threshold of social significance?' he asks, and replies, in essence, by questioning the validity of various scientific studies of garden-variety mystical experiences (Fales, 1996b, pp. 307–11). Fales concludes, though, that, 'the capacity for ecstatic experience is a natural human endowment ... [I]t would hardly be surprising if there were not sporadic occurrences of ecstasy which did not fit that picture: random effervescence, as it were, of the human potential for dissociative states' (p. 311). Fales suggests we look to brain physiology as a way of uncovering some reason for garden-variety mysticism. This reply will not do, however. We do not need valid scientific studies to know what is common knowledge, that there are many individuals, especially in religious contexts such as prayer and contemplation, who have theistic mystical experiences who do not fit the category of being a 'great mystic'. With the irrelevance of hopes for power, garden-variety mysticism severely challenge Fales's sociological explanation of mystical experiences of God.

My comments on 'garden-variety' mystics find confirmation in studies that have been done on the new 'spiritual awakening' of the late twentieth century in the United States (see Roof, 1993 and 1999; Wuthnow, 1998; and Wexler, 2000). While 'spirituality' encompasses more than what I mean in this study by 'mystical experience of God', the phenomenon of spirituality includes increased devotion to seeking mystical experiences, including theistic varieties. Robert Wuthnow, a leading American scholar of the sociology of religion, explains the spiritual renaissance in the United States by appeal to social factors affecting the empowered, privileged population more than the oppressed and marginalized. Due to social fragmentation, increased mobility, and a loss of anchoring in traditional religions, more and more Americans perceive themselves, in Wuthnow's terminology, no longer as spiritually 'dwelling' but as spiritually 'seeking' (Wuthnow, 1998, Chapter 1). Wuthnow sees spiritual seeking driven as well by complex social problems that the empowered feel increasingly inadequately equipped to do too much about. These include environmental pollution and desecration, hunger and poverty, the worldwide AIDS epidemic and crime. Seekers look to spirituality and mysticism to replace the disappointing promise of safe 'dwelling' in traditional religions.

Wuthnow's studies clash with the idea that mystical experience arises from within conditions of powerlessness, oppression or marginalization. Factors accounting for a turn to mystical experiences in late twentieth-century United States, for example accelerated mobility, disappointment with religion, and a frustrated, active social consciousness, relate to the empowered more than to the unempowered and underprivileged. Neither does the turn to mysticism provide social and political power of the kind involved in our sociological explanation. If anything, it is a turn away from social-political activity to ameliorate the effects of undesirable circumstances. So again, garden-variety mysticism counts against the present sociological explanation of theistic perceptions.

Problems with Fales's reductionist strategy   Let us return to the statement, (R), of the reductionist position as laid out in the previous chapter:

(a)   There is a set of naturalistic circumstances C, such that most (perhaps all) subjects who perceive God are in some C-circumstance.

(b)   Being in a C-circumstance gives reason to expect or suspect those subjects would have had God perceptions, even if their perceptions were illusory (e-reductionism), or being in a C-circumstance gives reason to expect or suspect those subjects had illusory God-perceptions (t-reductionism).

(c)   There is no set C1 of naturalistic circumstances, such that: most subjects who perceive God are in some C1-circumstance and being in a C1-circumstance counts significantly in favor of the subjects having had veridical experiences of God.

and:

(d)   A person's being in C does not give reason to expect or suspect the person's perceptions would be veridical, if God existed.

Now, when we apply clause (a) to Fales's sociological alternative, the relevant C-circumstance would be that subjects who have God-perceptions are in a position, and are aware of this as well, to use their mysticism to the advantage of their marginalized or otherwise oppressed group. This sociological explanation then will want to claim in (b), in accordance with Fales's t-reductionist intentions, that being in those circumstances shows that subjects had illusory God-perceptions. I imagine the idea is that we should suspect subjects of being led (unconsciously for the most part, I assume) by their desires for power to take some illusory experiences of theirs for genuine theistic perceptions. Let us pretend this is so. Now, then, according to clause (d), such a C-circumstance satisfies the reductionist program only if a person's being in it does not give reason to expect or suspect the person's perceptions would be veridical, if God existed. Here we meet a problem, for it is far from clear that this is so.

Imagine for a moment that all theistic mystics there ever were managed to achieve improvements for their marginalized or otherwise oppressed group by force of their mystical authority. Would this not be a reason to think God had indeed really appeared to them? After all, given the concept of God in mystical traditions it would be fitting and proper for God to appear to people to act through them for the relief of oppression and injustice.

In an earlier chapter I noted William Wainwright's contention that cross-checks of the validity of God-perceptions included checking whether the consequences of the experience were good for the mystic. The experience, that is, should be found to lead to or reinforce virtues such as wisdom, humility and charity in the life of the subject. Generally, acting for the good of one's oppressed group shows wisdom and charity. Acting in this way, therefore, should count in favor of the authenticity of mystical experience. A second test advanced by Wainwright was that a person's perceptions of God should prove 'fruitful and edifying' for others. If mystical experiences of God give subjects the power, courage and insight to help their oppressed group, that should count in favor of the validity of the experiences.

Hence, it would seem that the C-circumstances of our present sociological explanation do not easily fit requirement (d) of the reductionist program.

Before leaving Fales's sociological explanation, it is worth asking whether we really should want this explanation to succeed. On the one hand, it is a strength of a theory when it can explain data that were hitherto thought to be unrelated. Fales's sociological theory does well on that account. It explains spirit-possession and mystical experiences of God by one unified theory. On the other hand, it is a weakness of a theory when it explains disparate phenomena we think ought not to receive a common explanation. That will happen when we feel the theory overlooks crucial differences between phenomena, differences that defy assimilation to one another. Then a common theory will appear forced, artificial and superficial.

I suggest that one's willingness to accept a sociological explanation would likely be influenced by a prior rejection of the theistic explanation of God-perceptions. Then one would be attracted to giving one theory for what would be two hallucinatory types of experiences involving alleged intimate contact with an unseen being, here a spirit, there, God. One would be prepared for the deflation of God-perceptions as simply a variation on the discredited theme of intimate contact with an invisible being. The assimilation of theistic perceptions to spirit-possession would look rather attractive as a way to close the case on God-perceptions.

However, when we assume that the Argument from Perception establishes the initial evidential sufficiency of the theistic explanation, we should conclude differently. The evidence offered by the Argument from Perception counts against there being one theory for both spirit-possession and God-perceptions. Under these circumstances, the differences should count for more. In spirit possession a person is invaded and controlled by an alien force. In God-perceptions this is typically not the case. In spirit-possession the spirit can be driven out and the person freed by magical manipulations. No such practice exists for God-perceptions. Spirit-possession brings clear and immediate material gains to the subject; mystical experiences of God do not. In light of the Argument from Perception we have good reason to emphasize the differences and not the similarities.

I conclude that for all of the listed reasons we are justified in doubting that Fales's application of Lewis's theory to theistic experiences will be successful.

The Analogical Neuropsychological Explanation

The Theory

Psychological explanations of theistic experiences have had their champions for quite some time. Feurbach and Freud, for example, each advanced a psychological explanation for religious belief and by implication for religious experiences. None of these theories has met with general consent.[14] In the last decades of the twentieth century, a new generation of explanations, of a neuropsychological kind, has come to the fore. In this chapter I select two such theories for examination.

The first neuropsychological explanation grows out of a theory of mystical experience by C. Daniel Batson, Patricia Schoenrade and W. Larry Ventis (1993). Although these authors do not present the theory explicitly as a replacement for a theistic interpretation, it is natural to read it that way, as a truth-reductionist explanation. And although they present their theory as still in the speculative stage, it merits attention for the type of approach it represents and for its motivating a research program. Since the idea draws on an alleged analogy to psychological processes in creative problem solving, I will call this alternative explanation the explanation by analogy with creative problem solving, or for short the 'analogical explanation'.

The analogical explanation looks attractive because it means to compare religious experience with other cognitive processes, and makes use of theories about workings of the brain. Both these features promise an economy of explanation, assimilating religious experience to other modes of explanation. Since the analogical alternative pertains to religious experience in general, and not to theistic experience in particular, it requires supplementing by an explanation for why some people perceive God in particular, in their religious experiences. Nothing in the analogy to creative problem solving or the brain workings cited helps here, so this facet of the story will have to find explanation elsewhere. Perhaps the explanation would be cultural: people enmeshed in a theistic culture will interpret their religious experiences accordingly.

Batson et al. look to what they call 'reality-transforming' experiences as the key to understanding the nature of religious experiences. Specifically, they hope to gain understanding from an analogical approach, 'employing insights gained from psychological analyses of creativity' (p. 88). In doing so they adopt a methodology they attribute to William James, who thought 'the best approach is to focus on the most dramatic and intense experiences because in them one finds most clearly displayed the psychological processes also present in less dramatic experiences' (p. 81). The authors apparently have in mind the following passage from James's classic *The Varieties of Religious Experience* (1958, pp. 48–9):

I said in my former lecture that we learn most about a thing when we view it under a microscope, as it were, or in its most exaggerated form. This is as true of religious phenomena as of any other kind of fact. The only cases likely to be profitable enough to repay our attention will therefore be cases where the religious spirit is unmistakable and extreme ... It is with these more energetic cases that our sole business lies...

So here is their plan: to compare the dramatic breakthroughs of creative solutions to problems, to dramatic, 'energetic' mystical experiences. In doing so, they hope to come to an adequate psychological understanding of mystical experiences in general.

For this purpose, Batson et al. adopt the following scheme due to Graham Wallas, setting down four stages in the creative process of problem solving (Wallas, 1926, pp. 98–9):

1 *Preparation*: A period of struggle in which a person addresses their problem within the person's existing cognitive structures. Those structures prove inadequate for the solution of the problem, yet the person continues trying to make them work. The person gets the feeling of being trapped, with no way out of the problem.
2 *Incubation*: The attempt to solve the problem is given up. In doing so, the person unwittingly relaxes the hold of the existing cognitive structures.
3 *Illumination*: Here an entirely new cognitive organization emerges on the scene. New cognitive structures allow a new way of seeing the elements of the problem, leading to its solution. An insight arises: an 'Aha!' experience takes place.
4 *Verification*: The solution resulting from cognitive restructuring gets tested against experience and is found to work. The insight proves correct to the satisfaction of the subject.

The key idea is that of 'cognitive structures'. This will provide the link to the proposed neuropsychological understanding of mystical experiences. 'Cognitive structures,' the analogical theorists write, 'are conceptual dimensions on which we scale our experience; they allow us to compare one experience with another' (Batson et al., 1993, p. 90). Cognitive structures grant us our ability to classify and differentiate the contents of our experiences. To illustrate, our typical cognitive structures provide a grid for dimensions of color, size, weight and function. These dimensions are the 'framework in which reality is woven'. Of course, our cognitive structures include categories that are more complex as well.

Next, Batson et al. point out that cognitive structures are hierarchically arranged: 'To say that our cognitive structures are hierarchically arranged means that relatively specific dimensions are grouped under more general organizing principles, which are grouped under even more abstract and general organizing principles' (p. 92). For a simple example, our typical cognitive structures include particular shades of red, followed by the generic category of red, followed by color, followed by the category of a surface feature, all arranged in rising hierarchal gradations. Some of our problem solving requires organizing-principles at a level higher than the structural complexity we have so far enjoyed. Our hierarchical structure is too short, as it were. To progress we have to be able to undergo changes in our cognitive structures themselves, finding ourselves with new and taller hierarchal arrangements, giving us a more powerful way than earlier to organize the elements of the problem with which we began. In other cases, the hierarchal matrix must be restructured in order to provide different categories of classification.

In creative problem solving, one cognitive organization replaces another, the very framework within which we think is changed. More precisely, 'Creative thought may be defined as the process whereby one's cognitive structures are changed toward greater flexibility and adaptability through greater differentiation and integration' (1993, p. 94). 'Differentiation' refers to the ability to differentiate between items of thought, and 'integration' refers to the relationships between the dimensions of differentiation and the organizing principles and between organizing principles themselves. In creativity, the old organizing structures are seen as having limited application, and needing to give way to a more powerful cognitive grid. New information alone will not help us, because it will be absorbed into our existing inadequate cognitive thought processes. As long as cognitive transformation is not forthcoming, we are in 'preparation'.

It is in the relaxation of the attempt to deal with the problem, stopping coming up against an impenetrable wall, that is the stage of 'incubation' (sometimes called the 'bathtub stage'), that allows for the ability of a new grid of cognitive structures to emerge, of itself. When these do emerge, we arrive at the stage of 'illumination'. In verification, the solution proves correct to the satisfaction of the subject.

Batson et al. are attracted by the proposal that the creative sequence has a physiological basis in the structure of the brain. They endorse the view that the left hemisphere of the brain specializes in logical thought and language, while the right hemisphere specializes in perceptual organization and 'insight'. Some psychologists have proposed that the left hemisphere works within cognitive structures imposed on it, while the right hemisphere is responsible for the formation and maintenance of cognitive structures (see Ornstein, 1972).

During the stage of 'preparation', according to this suggestion, a person's attempts to solve the problem at hand are guided by left-hemisphere activity. Since the left-hemisphere thought cannot provide a new conceptual grid, the person gets stuck. When in 'incubation', the theory goes, the left-hemisphere activity is subdued, giving the right-hemisphere the possibility of reorganizing its cognitive structures. The insight achieved is actually a change in cognitive structuring. Passing to 'verification', the person returns to left-hemisphere application of the new conceptual grid.

Our authors propose to apply this theory of creativity to religious experience. Based on research conducted by various psychologists, they contend that many religious experiences display the same four-stage progression as creative problem solving:

1   *Preparation*: Religious experiences have their root in personal existential crises. Subjects try to work through their crises within their existing cognitive structures. This yields no satisfactory solution.
2   *Incubation*: Failing to solve one's existential crisis, one comes to despair or exhaustion. This brings to a relaxation of the effort to solve one's problem within one's existing cognitive structures.
3   *Illumination*: The person undergoes a transforming 'religious' or 'mystical' experience, one that issues in a new way of looking at the old problem. The new way of thinking 'transcends' the old based on the old cognitive structures.
4   *Verification*: The transforming experience gives rise to a 'new life'. The new 'theology', a corollary of the redeeming experience, yields a new 'sanctification'. The person enjoys a loss of worry, a sense of the lucidity of reality, and returns to the world with assurance from within a new perspective.

In citing this four-stage process, we do not yet obtain an alternative to the theistic understanding of mystical experiences of God. The element of replacing the theistic understanding comes in now. The proposed cognitive analogy between creative problem solving and mystical experience allegedly points to a common neurophysiological grounding, namely a shift from left- to right-hemisphere processing. This change may account therefore for the sense of 'transcendence' in religious experiences. 'Perhaps,' say Batson et al., 'because it involves cognitive transcendence, the new vision often seems to come from a transcendent realm outside oneself' (1993, p. 104).

Thus, a subject may seem to experience a transcendent reality, when in fact experiencing instead the switch from thinking within a given cognitive structure (left-hemisphere), to a meta-level, as it were, where cognitive structures are determined (right-hemisphere). The experience has a tingle of a 'going beyond', explaining the subject's sense of 'transcendence', a sense that gets (mis-) interpreted in religious terms.

Batson and friends refer sympathetically to the idea that with the analogical theory we could explain as well the so-called 'ineffability', or indescribability of a religious experience. They quote approvingly Jerome Frank who writes that some researchers believe that the 'transcendental experience' is mediated by the right hemisphere, the one concerned with patterns and emotions, in contrast to the analytic and verbal left hemisphere. This would account for the ineffability of the religious experience (p. 106). Fenwick (1996, pp. 167–77) took this position.

The idea is this. When having a religious experience, a person's brain shifts from left- to right-hemisphere dominance. When the right-hemisphere dominates, there is a sense of experience not providing articulation in words or concepts, that being the task of the left-hemisphere. This accounts, then, for the feeling that a religious experience is 'beyond description'.

To summarize, on the analogical theory the sense of perception of a transcendent reality is proposed (tentatively, albeit) to be really the person's experiencing the 'transcendent' feel of the shift from left- to right-hemisphere dominance. The person feels a sense of 'ascent' from the existing cognitive grid to a level wherein the grid is changed and reorganized. Because of acculturation, perhaps, a person is induced to identify what he or she experiences with God, rather than as something else. However, that is not the best identification of what the person perceives then. The theistic explanation of God-perceptions is superceded.

Evaluation of the Analogical Theory

As noted, Batson et al. state that their theory is still speculative. I should point out as well that some neural researchers have argued against applying the hemispheric-switch theory to mystical episodes.[15] In addition, not all creative problem solving comes with the transcendent feeling attributed to mystical experiences. If the hemispheric switch were supposed to characterize both types of experiences, the creative and the mystical, the sense of the transcendence would typify all creativity as well. So on empirical grounds alone the analogical explanation might not come up to standard. However my interest here is not only in the empirical adequacy of the theory. I am also interested in the philosophical question of whether the proposed explanation would have the potential, if empirically supported, to serve as an alternative explanation of purported theistic perceptions.

My answer is that I doubt whether the analogical explanation could replace the theistic understanding of God-perceptions, because I question the methodological approach from the very start. Recall that Batson et al. adopt a methodology they attribute to William James, that 'the best approach is to focus on the most dramatic and intense experiences because in them one finds most clearly displayed the psychological processes also present in less dramatic experiences'. I see no reason to accept this methodological starting point. In *The Varieties of Religious Experience*, James skews the study of religious experience toward the dramatic and one-time events by unjustifiably focusing on conversion experiences. These are invariably first-time experiences for the subject, radically different from any prior experience of the person. By so selecting his material, James has not shone light on all mystical or theistic experiences. On the contrary, James has given inordinate weight to the dramatic and the new in mystical experience. He fails entirely to capture experiences that occur in the quiet of 'normal mysticism'.[16]

By 'normal mysticism', I mean to refer to what occurs in the ongoing life of a person. Normal mysticism manifests, for example, in contemplative prayer in various religions, and in various religious activities. It can also characterize a person's rather steady experiential frame of mind. It can even apply to 'professional' mystics. The experiences of Teresa of Avila, for example, can be quite dramatic at times, to say the least, but are not conversion experiences and do not occur in conjunction with a new insight into a personal problem. They are part of a series of experiences over a long period in her life. In the analogical theory, we have been given no reason to think that normal mysticism involves an experience of hemispheric switching. For this reason the proposal of Batson et al. would be severely limited, even if correct. The theory would not account for the experiences of normal mysticism.

Because of their focus on first time, 'conversion' experiences, the analogical theorists give inordinate place to the existence of a personal problem before the experience, that the experience allegedly solves. Evidence for the problem-solving assumption comes from quotations by James of people's descriptions of the context in which they had their first mystical experience. However, if we reject the exclusive concentration on conversion, we lose the reason for endorsing the personal-problem-solving analogy of mystical experiences. In ongoing normal mysticism, the theory lacks plausibility. We would have to believe that a 'normal mystic' was solving a new personal problem almost daily or weekly, via mystical experience. Alternatively, we would be asked to accept that frequency of experiences was a sign of ongoing attempts to solve the same personal problem. Neither of these is convincing.

I conclude that the analogy model does not do justice to the variety of circumstances in which people perceive God.

Unfortunately, the analogical theory commits a mistake quite commonly made when thinking about mystical experiences. The more dramatic and bizarre mystical episodes attract attention and somehow become the standard for people's thinking about mysticism. The normal mystical experiences are not taken seriously into account. I trace the propensity for this error to William James's book on mystical experience and the stated methodological principle governing that work.

The inclination to equate mystical experience with the dramatic and bizarre is manifest when a work on consciousness and the brain contains a chapter entitled, 'Madness and Mysticism' (Rose, 1989, Chapter 12). In a less pronounced way we find it with Robert Elwood, a scholar of mysticism, who seems quite cognizant of normal mysticism. Nonetheless he writes of the 'structure' of mystical experience as including, the 'unexpectedness' of the mystic's encounter with the transcendent, a sudden 'flash of absolute power or ecstasy', and an 'afterglow' (Elwood, 1999, p. 76). Here too a favoring of the intensely dramatic is clearly at work. A type of mystical experience available in contemplative prayer, for example, need not fit this description. An experience in that context might be 'unexpected' in the sense that one cannot plan to have it, but is hardly unexpected in the sense of being totally surprising. In addition, flashes of ecstatic power need not happen in normal mysticism.

The same attraction for the dramatic and bizarre may motivate other theories concerning the brain and mystical experiences. For example, research on epilepsy has led several researchers to pin their hopes for understanding mystical experiences on activity in the temporal lobes of the brain, where epileptic conditions are located (Bear and Fedio, 1977; Geschwind, 1983; and Persinger, 1984 and 1987). In fact, one study by Dewhurst and Beard sought a correlation – and found one – between temporal lobe epilepsy and sudden conversion experiences (Dewhurst and Beard, 1970). I suggest that the attractiveness of thinking that micro-seizures would significantly explain mystical experiences reflects a preoccupation with the more dramatic and attention-grabbing forms of such experiences, such as conversion experiences, to the detriment of normal mysticism.[17]

What of those episodes where dramatic conversion does take place following failure to solve an existential problem? Would the analogical proposal offer a good alternative for a theistic explanation of those episodes? On its behalf, we could point to theoretical advantages in being able to account for both theistic experiences and 'creativity experiences' in terms of the same shift from left- to right-hemispheric processing. On the other hand, a theoretical disadvantage would result from splitting off the explanation of dramatic conversion episodes from that of normal mystical ones. If the same experience of transcendence occurs in both conversion experiences and normal mysticism, it is better not to ascribe different factors in the causality of the two.[18] Accordingly, the theoretical advantages would be dubious for a restricted application of the analogical argument.

Eugene d'Aquili and Andrew Newberg

The Theory

I close this chapter with an examination of a sophisticated neuropsychological theory of mystical experiences that has attracted much attention. This is the theory of Eugene d'Aquili and Andrew Newberg (1993, 1999 and 2000; see also Laughlin et al., 1990). While the theory has undergone some development and changes, its main outline follows.

Focusing first on meditative mystical states, d'Aquili and Newberg's theory proposes the prefrontal area of the brain, especially the lateral convexity of the frontal lobe, as the locus of special brain activity during mystical episodes. (In their presentations, the authors provide excellent figures of the brain to guide the reader along. Readers are referred to those diagrams for clarification of the terminology employed here.) The theory proposes understanding mystical states as involving 'deafferentiation' or the cutting off of neural input into various structures of the nervous system. The theory then distinguishes between 'passive meditation' and 'active meditation' (1993, p. 186).

Passive meditation is characterized by the intent to clear the mind of content, as much as possible. The theory proposes that this intention sets off an intricate system of deafferentiation within the brain that 'results in ecstatic and blissful feelings via intense stimulation of structures both in the lateral hypothalamus and in the median forebrain area' (p. 187). A consequent neutralizing of the posterior superior parietal lobule, responsible for spatial coordination of incoming stimuli, creates a sense of 'pure space' experienced as absolute unity or wholeness (p. 189). Together, the patterns set up in the brain in passive meditation create an overwhelming experience of 'absolute unitary being'. At this point two alternative continuations of the brain processes are possible, depending on how impulses sent out from the involved brain structures affect other parts of the brain, particularly the limbic structures. In one alternative, a reinforcing of the lateral hypothalamic discharge reinforces the initial ecstasy of the experience and, on the other, the initial ecstasy is followed by a 'deep and profound quiescence' by way of a return to dominance of the ventromedial hypothalamic structures.

At this point, the theory introduces the difference between theistic and non-theistic mystical experiences (p. 190):

> If the first situation occurs, AUB [absolute unitary being] is not only experienced initially as ecstasy, but the ecstasy is maintained throughout the period of contemplation. If the second situation occurs, then after the initial moment of ecstasy, AUB is experienced as a deep quiescent Void or Nirvana. We would suggest that the first situation tends to be interpreted personally (after the fact) as the immediate experience or union with God. In the second case, the experience of AUB tends to be interpreted impersonally, as the peace and emptiness of the absolute ground of being.

In a later paper, the difference between theistic and non-theistic experiences is put somewhat differently (d'Aquili and Newberg, 2000, p. 43):

> In AUB [absolute unitary being] there is no extension of space or duration or time. If this state is suffused with positive effect, it is interpreted, after the fact, as the experience of God or the *Unio Mystica*. If it is suffused with neutral effect, it is experienced nonpersonally as the Void, or Nirvana, of Buddhism.[19]

The difference, again, gets traced back to a difference in neuropsychological goings-on.

In 'active meditation', the subject intends to focus on a mental image or on an external object. The d'Aquili-Newberg theory describes a brain-story comparable to that for passive mediation, resulting in the falling away of the subject-object distinction and the emergence of absolute unitary being.

Next, the theory attends to 'lesser mystical states', those falling short of the absolute unitary being experience, including those that occur spontaneously, without meditative preparation. d'Aquili and Newberg posit that while in meditative states there is 'maximal stimulation', in lesser religious states we are dealing with 'mild to moderate' stimulation of certain circuits in the lateral hypothalamus. This generates 'a mild to moderate fear accompanied by a sense of exaltation. This, then, is the complex often referred to as 'religious awe' (d'Aquili and Newberg, 1993, p. 195). 'Numinous' experiences and Otto's experience of *Mysterium Tremendum* are further explained by variations of deafferentiation, the cutting off of neural input into various structures of the nervous system. The theory leaves open for further study just what could trigger sudden deafferentiation, with no preceding meditative concentration.

The strength of the d'Aquili-Newberg theory lies in its explanation of a continuum of mystical experiences by a common type of explanation, involving specific parts of the brain and their deafferentiation. It explains theistic and non-theistic experiences, and meditative and non-meditative experiences, including spontaneous episodes. It thus gives an economic way of explaining a wide range of mystical experiences, including theistic ones. In a further elaboration of the theory, d'Aquili and Newberg propose that certain parts of the brain function in similar ways across aesthetic, spiritual and mystical states, thus giving the theory power to explain an even more impressive variety of experiences (d'Aquili and Newberg, 2000, p. 43).

Now d'Aquili and Newberg themselves caution against a reductionist reading of their theory (1993, p. 197):

> To maintain that the reality of a person's 'objective' experience of God is reducible to neurochemical flux and nothing more may be equivalent to maintaining that the person's experience of the 'objective' reality of the sun, earth, and the air we breathe is reducible to neurochemical flux ... Perhaps we need to maintain an attitude of humility, rather than of arrogant presumption that our knowledge of neurophysiology can give us intrinsic knowledge of the relationship between 'reality' and consciousness, whether in its baseline or more esoteric forms.

D'Aquili and Newberg are saying that their neuropsychological theory cannot deny the objectivity of a God-experience. They cannot invoke the theory to conclude that God is not the perceived object of such experiences. A theory describing neural goings-on would no more show there were no genuine experiences of God or that we had no reason to think there were, than do unique neural processes for perceiving physical objects count against the genuine perception of physical objects. In both cases, presumably, we will have described no more than the way perceptions of the respective objects are processed in the brain.

Nevertheless, the d'Aquili-Newberg theory does carry reductionist pressure concerning experiences specifically of God. Here's why. The above quote allows that something, rather than nothing, may serve as the object of mystical experiences of God. However, this is consistent with the object of God-perceptions being something far less specific than 'God', with the 'God-details' supplied by brain goings-on or by the subjective interpretation of the person. Indeed the theory posits that neurophysiological factors (undoubtedly influenced by salient cultural factors) will determine whether mediators think they are experiencing God, or something else. In addition, the theory suggests that in 'lesser experiences' subjects simply interpret 'religious feelings' theistically. These elements of the theory raise questions about the objectivity of claiming that a perception was specifically of God. Perhaps at best the perception only of an amorphous 'reality' is objective while all the rest is supplied by the brain and cultural conditioning. That the present theory subsumes perceptions of God under a broad canopy of human experiences speaks in favor of reducing perceptions of God at best to the perception of a 'reality' describable in different ways, depending on how the brain attends to it. So the theory carries reductionist weight against thinking that God, in particular, is the object of theistic experiences.

The neuropsychological theory of d'Aquili and Newberg seems to pass the bar of high-level theoretical explanatory power. Because it explains such an imposing range of experiences, it poses an attractive, albeit restricted, reductionist alternative to the theistic understanding of God-perceptions.

Evaluation of the d'Aquili-Newberg Theory

Some philosophers of religion would be willing to accept the restricted reductionist implications of the d'Aquili-Newberg theory. They would rest content with the notion that in both theistic and non-theistic mystical experiences, subjects perceive one and the same reality, here perceived as God, there as the 'Void' or 'Brahman'. One way to explicate this position would be by way of John Hick's 'pluralist hypothesis'. In this hypothesis Hick posits the 'Real' as an essentially unknowable object in itself, manifesting different faces or 'personae' to different cultures and at different times (Hick, 1989). The Real in itself is neither personal nor impersonal, these categories being imposed upon the Real in the act of perception and cognition, issuing out of different cultural contexts. When perceived in one way, the Real is perceived as God, when perceived another way, as Brahman.

Religions, for Hick, are human responses to the Real, grounded in the respective cultural 'faces' imposed on the Real in experience, with the task of directing human hearts toward the Real and away from selfish interests. Experiences of the 'faces' of the Real are adequate to the religious life when they adequately serve the purpose of educating believers to strive to be directed toward the Real rather than directed toward their own needs and desires.

Hick could square d'Aquili and Newberg's theory with the pluralist hypothesis, by maintaining that cultural learning determines the way religious experience plays itself out in the brain. Theistic acculturation will cause the brain to reinforce lateral hypothalamic discharge, producing a theistic experience, while non-theistic religious training will bring about dominance of the ventromedial hypothalamic structures, and a corresponding non-theistic experience.

Not all theistic philosophers, however, are happy with Hick's position, and I have argued against it elsewhere (Gellman, 1997, Chapter Four). For a defender of a theistic explanation of God-perceptions of this type, the restricted reductionist implications of the d'Aquili-Newberg theory remain on the agenda.

A way for such theists to take issue with the restricted reductionist ramifications of the theory would be to point out its failure to deal adequately with the phenomenological content of theistic mystical experiences. The theory fails to take seriously enough the perceptual character of mystical experiences of God. Instead, it treats such experiences as composed entirely of a cluster of subjective feelings waiting to be interpreted by the subject as a perceptual episode. Hence, the theory asserts that whether meditating subjects experience God or the Void depends entirely upon whether they feel continued ecstasy or a deep quiescence, each of the latter nothing more than a feeling. Non-meditating subjects, too, according to d'Aquili and Newberg, experience nothing other than various dosages of feelings of fear and exaltation, that they then treat as perceptual data. The theory misses the perceptual character of mystical experiences of God.

As noted in my characterization of theistic mystical experiences, the phenomenal content of a mystical experience of God carries a subject-object structure. A subject senses being 'appeared-to'. It is not merely a matter of feelings. Such experiences often do involve heightened affective states and feelings. However, a mystical experience is not to be identified with these. The d'Aquili-Newberg theory does not account for the perceptual, subject-object character of many mystical experiences of God. Consequently, its neuropsychological tale cannot be the whole story. At best, it accounts for the physiological basis for the affective concomitants of mystical experiences.

This objection, however, does not touch deeply enough the philosophical issues raised by a neuropsychological theory of this type. To get to the heart of the problem of the restricted reductionist challenge let us pretend we have a confirmed theory like the d'Aquili-Newberg one, describing what goes on inside the brain when God-perceptions occur, one that has uncovered perceptual-type brain-mechanisms as the ground for mystical experiences. Suppose the theory possesses strong, comprehensive explanatory power, similar to the d'Aquili-Newberg explanation. Would we be required then to accept its reductionist implications that only some general 'reality' could be inferred as object and not something as specific as God? Here is a reason for thinking we would not.

As I have argued in Chapter Three, the Argument from Perception grants an initial evidential case for the theistic interpretation of God-perceptions. So we may take our imaginary neuropsychological theory as succeeding in describing no more than how God gets into our consciousness. We should have expected, after all, that a non-sensory perception of the sort God-perceptions purport to be would involve unique brain events. God-perceptions would not likely proceed by way of ordinary brain processes. Furthermore, a theory can do no more than tell us what happens in the brain when a mystical experience of God takes place. It cannot tell us this happens while God is not really appearing to the subject or that an explanation in terms of brain processes defeats a theistic explanation. We should reject any attempt to conclude that the ultimate cause for a theory's favored brain events is altogether internal to the organism and internal especially to the brain. Instead, we can happily accept the favored brain events and ascribe their very occurrence to an external ultimate cause, God.

The situation is similar with the brain and physical objects. Recognizing that the brain works a certain way when a subject perceives a physical object, we do not deny that an external physical object is the ultimate cause of the perception. The only access any of us has to physical objects is via perception. We take the perceptual character of the experience as grounds for believing there to be an external object. The same with God-perceptions. We are justified in taking their perceptual character as indicating an external ultimate cause, God.[20] So a suitably revised neuropsychological theory should not threaten the validity of God-perceptions. Here is a response to this objection.

The objection fails to take into account a serious difference between physical object perceptions and God-perceptions, a difference that seriously impugns the contended parallel between them. In the case of sensory perception, we have clear evidence for the existence of a cause originating from a point external to the brain. Take vision for example. We can trace the impinging of light onto the retina from outside the organism, can follow the impulses through the ganglion cells that converge on the retina, onward to the optic nerve, on to the optic tracts of the posterior part of the forebrain, and so forth. We thus possess clear empirical grounding for a visual stimulus outside the brain.

True enough our access to the visual story is exclusively through our sensory-perceptions, so in the end we have nothing to rely on but the perceptual structure of our experiences. Nevertheless, within the circle of perceptual evidence, we possess collaborating evidence about an external source and how it gets into us, the story about light and how it gets to the brain, that strengthens the sheer perceptual structure of our visual experiences. The same holds for our other sense modalities.

No such story exists for God-perceptions. We have no parallel neuropsychological story about how God gets into the organism and the brain, because our imaginary theory tells us only what happens inside the brain during mystical episodes. The theory would not have discovered any 'God receptors' analogous to the retina or the inner-ear sense receptors. A theistic interpretation of God-perceptions would thus lack cohering empirical backing for the validity of its perceptions that sensory perceptions enjoy. This would make it easier for our imagined neuropsychological theory to overcome the weight of the evidence from the perceptual, subject-object nature of God-perceptions in favor of a broadly comprehensive theory that locates the ultimate cause of these perceptions in a story internal to the subject, complemented by cultural influences. The reductionist pressures abide. Here is an objection to this reply.

The absence of 'God receptors' would count not at all in favor of replacing the theistic understanding of God-perceptions with our imaginary neuropsychological explanation. Perceptual receptors that feed into the brain are to be expected and sought for when dealing with a physical stimulus, but not with non-physical stimuli as in mystical experiences of God. Physical stimuli are at a physical distance from the brain and so we need receptors to carry the stimuli, physically, to the brain. God, however, does not exist at a physical distance from the brain. Furthermore, God can act directly upon the brain to bring about the relevant processes for a subject to perceive God. Therefore, the absence of God-receptors analogous to sensory receptors does nothing to enhance the reductionist force of our imaginary neuropsychological explanation of mystical experiences of God. We remain with the previous point that a story about what happens in the brain during God-perceptions does not have the power, in itself, to undermine the theistic understanding of those perceptions.

I believe this objection to be correct. However, the theistic defender should not exaggerate the victory. All the argument shows is that not just any neuropsychological explanation would have reductionist power against the Argument from Perception. It does not follow that no neuropsychological theory could be successful at offering an alternative explanation. I can envisage a theory of this category that would be seriously damaging to a theistic understanding of God-perceptions. To see this, recall from the previous chapter how truth-reductionists, who deny the validity of God-perceptions, might typically argue. They would argue that there was a set of naturalistic circumstances C, such that most (perhaps all) subjects who perceived God were in some C-circumstance, and that being in a C-circumstance gave reason to expect or suspect those subjects had inauthentic God-perceptions. As long as there were no additional circumstances that most subjects who perceived God were in that counted in favor of the veridicality of their experience, and provided that a person's being in C did not give reason to expect or suspect the person's perceptions would be veridical, we should conclude that the experiences were not veridical.

I gave this example: Suppose we discovered that people who had mystical experiences of God had taken mescaline before their experiences. It simply does not square with God's alleged character that God would appear to all and only people who had taken mescaline. Nothing singles out mescaline users for the special treatment implied by their having really experienced God. Hence, given the fulfillment of the other conditions in the reductionist's argument, people who seemed to perceive God most likely did not have veridical perceptions of God, although they might have had, for all we know, an experience of some mystical reality.

Similarly there could be a neuropsychological account of mystical experiences of God that made it implausible to believe people really did come into experiential contact with God. The implausibility would follow from the nature of the specific brain mechanisms involved and the unlikelihood, given God's alleged character, of that being the way God would reveal to human beings. The brain mechanisms would thus be of a sort we should expect not to exist were the experiences veridical. For example, suppose researchers showed that mystical experiences of God were always dependent on a minor brain-abnormality caused by people, appropriately genetically disposed, having been fed certain diets in childhood, while the other conditions of the reductionist argument were met. God could choose, I suppose, to get into people's consciousness in that way, influencing events in order to appear to the right people, as it were. Yet such a discovery would provide implausible necessary conditions for mystical experiences of God. After all, why should God visit only people with such histories and such genetic dispositions? It makes little sense. Hence, given the other conditions in the reductionist argument, we should conclude that it was unlikely that people had genuinely experienced God. If that seems too strong, at least there would be good reason to think that the evidence in favor of the genuineness of God-experiences had been seriously undermined.

The d'Aquili-Newberg theory does not introduce any element that would help the reductionist challenge a theistic understanding of mystical experiences of God, because it introduces no neuropsychological mechanism that would be an implausible candidate for how God gets into the brain. Further research into the neuropsychology of these experiences might produce a plausible reductionist account. Perhaps Persinger's theory has potentials in this direction (see Persinger, 1993 and 1987). At present, however, researchers, such as d'Aquili and Newberg on the one hand and Persinger on the other, are divided on the relevant brain-locales and mechanisms involved in mystical experience. So it is too early to decide in favor of a sweeping neuropsychological reduction of mystical experiences of God.

A neuropsychological explanation of just some God-perceptions, say the more intense, dramatic ones, could take its place alongside other explanations that satisfactorily explain other episodes of God-perceptions. In this way, an accumulation of alternative explanations could pose a serious challenge to the theistic understanding of God-perceptions by explaining away an increasing number of such experiences. At what point the scale tips away from the theistic explanation to naturalistic ones is difficult to determine. In any case, the neuropsychological challenge appears potentially the most serious there is to the evidential case for the validity of mystical experiences of God.

This concludes my investigation into the three representative reductionist explanations I have chosen. While I have shown the shortcomings of these three, I hope I have contributed to an understanding of what it would take for a reductionist alternative to be successful.

Notes

1   Fales has made this clear to me in private correspondence.
2   Lewis has elaborated his theory in Lewis, 1986 and 1989.
3   In my depiction of the life of Jacob Boehme, I have relied upon Jones, 1914, Chapters 9–12, and Weeks, 1991. Below I take issue with some of Weeks's conclusions.
4   One could argue that for a similar reason Boehme stayed quiet for such a long time. He might have acted cautiously because of the perceived danger to him due to his beliefs.
5   An excellent survey of the *nagidim* can be found in the introduction to David son of Joshua son of Abraham Maimonides, 1987. Those who held the position of *nagid* were known by their father's name, and not by their mother's.
6   For a profile of Abraham, see Goiten, 1988, pp. 476–96.
7   Abraham had a son, Obadyah, who was also a practicing Sufi and the author of a mystical work, *The Treatise of the Pool*. However Obadyah was not a *nagid*.
8   The new research includes Rosman, 1996; Ettinger, 1991; Rapaport-Albert, 1996; and Etkes, 1988 and 1996.
9   For the Baal Shem Tov's innovation in prayer, see Jacobs, 1973, Chapter 6.
10 For the life and thought of Rabbi Kook, see Ish-Shalom, 1993.
11 I have written about R. Kook's mystical poetry in Gellman, 1994.
12 See, for example, Rasmussan, 1995; and Sered, 1994.
13 See, for example, Hardy, 1980.
14 For an excellent summary of criticism of these proposals, see Davis, 1989.
15 See Pagano and Warrenburg, 1983.
16 I borrow the term 'normal mysticism' from Max Kadushin, 1978, who uses the term in a somewhat different sense than I do here.
17 Persinger, 1993 and 1987, however, has studied a connection between less dramatic experiences, such as meditation, and temporal lobe activity.
18 A diehard might add the following: the alleged equation between creativity and alleged theistic experience could just as easily be read from right to left. That is, we could just as easily assimilate creativity to mystical experience, as do the reverse. We would then take the evidence for the validity of mystical experience as evidence as well that God inspires creative solutions to problems!
19 Austin, 1998, has provided an entirely different account of non-theistic mystical experience, specifically in Zen meditation.
20 I do not mean to be arguing that the evidential case for God perceptions is on a par with the case for sensory perception. I have discussed the evidential differential between the two in Chapter Three. Presently I am arguing only that the structure of the evidential inference is similar in the two cases.

Chapter 6

Gender and Mystical Experience of God

Feminist thinkers have voiced moral, epistemological and theological views strongly challenging to the enterprise I have undertaken in this work. In the present chapter, I propose to engage these critical positions.

I will be discussing three feminist critiques. The first says that the usual male philosopher's treatment of mystical experience, of which my treatment might be a good example, perpetrates or implicitly encourages social and political injustice toward women. This I shall call the 'moral critique'.

A second criticism states that concepts like 'evidence', 'experience', 'perception' and 'rationality', all central to my conceptual apparatus, are social constructions developed by dominating white, upper middle-class males, reflecting their point of view to the exclusion of all others, most pointedly, women. Had I implicitly assumed these categories in my investigation, I thereby would have biased my epistemology from the start. This is the 'epistemological critique'.

The third criticism claims that contemporary treatments of mystical experience display an androcentric bias toward the nature of such experiences and their alleged content. The God allegedly revealed in mystical theistic experiences is a patriarchal God who fits men's wildest dreams of independence and domination. It is not a woman's God. My approach, if proposing to look at the evidence from what men count as theistic experience, and sanctioning a male God-concept, threatens to sanctify this theological bias against women. I call this the 'theological critique'.

The Moral Critique

Grace Jantzen has expounded an extensive critique of the way contemporary male philosophers of religion allegedly treat 'mysticism' (Jantzen, 1994 and 1995). Jantzen's major problem is with the purported attempt to make 'mysticism' no more than, or most centrally, a matter of the 'private' psychological episodes of a solitary person. Scholars, she says, see 'mysticism essentially in terms of intense, private, subjective experiences', and believe that 'it is these experiences whose significance must be studied if we are to grasp the meaning and value of mysticism' (1995, p. 6).

What is unjust or otherwise immoral about this? There seem to be two separate charges. The first is that by focusing upon private, individual experiences in mysticism, the philosopher ignores social and structural ills of society. Preoccupation with private experiences strengthens the neglect of social injustices, from which, among others, women suffer.

Jantzen deplores the resurgence of interest in 'spirituality' in Western countries, signifying to her a turning inward to oneself as a way of coping with one's problems, including one's suffering from repression and injustice. People should be focusing instead on correcting the structural faults in the social structure in which their personal problems arise in the first place. From a feminist point of view, this is deeply distressing because, by putting the emphasis on the personal and the private, 'the structures of injustice' are being reinforced, especially the structures that impose injustice upon women (p. 20).

So too philosophical investigations of mysticism dealing with mysticism as though it were entirely or mainly a matter of internal psychological attitudes, inhibits the advance of social change for justice. Jantzen writes that 'feminists deplore a division between the personal and the political, and are justly suspicious of any philosophical discussion which purports to be neutral with regard to issues of justice' (p. 11). Philosophers should be looking instead at the phenomenon of 'mysticism' in its social ramifications and should expose the injustice to women in both the history and scholarly treatment of the phenomenon. 'The net result,' says Jantzen about philosophers' treatment of mysticism, 'whatever the intention of the authors and compilers, is the reinforcement of the societal status quo, as intellectual and religious energy is pored into an exploration of private religiosity rather than into social and political action for change' (p. 21).

Jantzen's second charge is specific to injustice toward women. She argues that, in former days, mysticism comprised an important social-political phenomenon, serving as a source of power and social influence for mystics and their followers. Because of its power-potential, claims Jantzen, women were historically marginalized as mystics. The rare woman who did get recognized as a mystic, owed this largely to ecclesiastic sponsorship by men, to having been 'adopted' by male mystics.

Jantzen claims that in recent times, at least in Western countries, religion and mysticism have become much less of a public force than they used to be. Specifically, the 'vocation' of being a mystic carries far less social and political authority than it did, say, in medieval times. Mysticism has become 'private'. For Jantzen, the 'privatization' of religion and mysticism goes hand in hand with a new willingness to count women as mystics. Why? Because prominently including women as mystics in the transformed situation feeds into the desire to relegate women to the realm of the private, and thereby deny them access to positions of power and social influence. Here is how Jantzen puts her reasoning (pp. xv–xvi):

> Religion has been discarded as a public force ... At the same time, religion, and especially religious experience, has become far more available to women – women who, in idealisation though not in reality, are also private, and are the

primary keepers of house and home. A connection can be traced between the domestication of women and the domestication of religion such that claims to religious experience become permissible for women in direct proportion to the decline of overt importance of religion.

Philosophers who treat mysticism as a private experience of a solitary subject, thereby reinforce the relegation of women to the margins of power.

The synchronic process of the privatization of religious experience and the admission of women into the circle of legitimate mystics also accounts, by Jantzen's lights, for the emphasis ever since William James, on the so-called 'ineffability' of mystical experiences. James took 'ineffability' as a distinguishing mark of mystical experience as opposed to other forms of conscious awareness. Here's how James characterized ineffability in *The Varieties of Religious Experience* (James, 1958, pp. 292–3):

> *Ineffability*. – The handiest of the marks by which I classify a state of mind as mystical is negative. The subject of it says that it defies expression, that no adequate report of its contents can be given in words ... In this peculiarity mystical states are more like states of feeling than like states of intellect.

More recently, the researchers of mysticism, Pahnke and Richards, have included the ineffability claim prominently in their mystical characterization of LSD experiences, as a claim about the inadequacy of language itself to contain or reflect such experiences (Pahnke and Richards, 1966). For Jantzen, setting up mystical experiences to be ineffable removes them from the realm of rational discourse, placing them instead into the realm of the emotions (1995, p. 344). That in turn implies removing mysticism from the traditional centers of political and social power, where 'reason' rules. So the stress on ineffability contributes to the political marginalizing of women, by gerrymandering mysticism to include women and thus socially disempower them.

Jantzen's critique applies with full measure to the discussions in this book. I have devoted the inquiry entirely to the evidential value of private, mystical experiences of God, without considering the wider issues of patriarchal repression and social injustice intertwined with mysticism and with its scholarly treatment. It follows that my enterprise shares the allegedly unjust intentions and consequences of what Jantzen takes to be typical of contemporary male treatments of mysticism. Jantzen's critique finds its mark here as well.

Reply: Mystical Experience and Privacy

I agree that there have been, and do remain, serious injustices toward women by male philosophers and scholars when acting in their profession. These injustices occur at the level of the academic life of philosophy as well as in the choice of philosophical topics and their treatment within the profession.

It is good and proper for women and men philosophers to work toward full justice for women in philosophy. Laudably, women philosophers and historians have been correcting a relative neglect of women's perspectives on mysticism. Jantzen has delineated the tribulations of women in medieval Christian mysticism (Jantzen, 1995), and she and others have brought to our attention outstanding women mystics, such as Hildegard of Bingen and Julian of Norwich (see Beer, 1993, and Brunn and Epiney-Burgard, 1989). Scholarship toward the end of the twentieth century has raised our appreciation for what are often the distinctive modes of experience of women mystics. We are now learning from feminist scholars and others, for example, of the importance of the aesthetic imagination in mystical experience (see Classen, 1998, Chapter One, and Borchert, 1994). In addition, women philosophers and theologians, including Jantzen, have been developing feminist philosophies of religion and feminist theologies. I welcome these new developments for enriching my understanding of the religious impulse and awareness of the varieties of mysticism hardly noticed by William James and others.

Nevertheless, I question the contention that treating mysticism as 'private' reflects or colludes with a desire to repress women by consigning them to a private sphere, at home and with the family. Jantzen cites little empirical data to support this claim other than pointing to a claimed correlation between religion becoming more private and men allegedly displaying an increased readiness to acknowledge women's mysticism. Without more supporting evidence, it is hard to know how to assess the claim that treating of mysticism as private is prejudicial to women. Women have suffered and continue to suffer greatly from misogynist behavior and oppressive social structures. However, whether a particular phenomenon has anti-women repercussions, let alone is motivated by misogyny, must be substantiated independently.

My main issue with Jantzen's thesis, though, is that because some philosophers choose to investigate the epistemology of mystical experiences, as I do, this need not indicate that they take the experiential psychological states of the mystic as of 'fundamental importance'. Neither need it imply a denial of justice to women in the spheres of mysticism or religion. A philosopher may happily agree that a number of features of mysticism are important and worth studying. In particular, I appreciate that mysticism has been an important social phenomenon, having important effects on social movements and political power. What interests me professionally, however, is the epistemology of mystical experiences. Sociologists and political theorists, among others, will examine the social and political aspects of mysticism. Epistemologists of religion will investigate the epistemology of mystical experiences.

I believe it important to have a good understanding of the evidential situation concerning mystical experiences. Doing so bears on the question of whether God exists, what God is like, if existing, and whether it is rational to believe in God. This does not mean that I regard 'mysticism' solely or mainly as a private phenomenon or that no other aspects of it deserve to be studied.

It might be said in response that as a philosopher one is free to choose to approach mysticism in other ways, including from an angle that would not be prejudicial to women. The failure to do so by treating mysticism as a private matter, and ignoring the repressive consequences of doing so, is prejudicial to women and therefore culpable. In reply, I suggest we make a distinction between two senses of 'private' experience.

Two Senses of 'Private'

In one sense, mystical experience is 'private' in that it involves an internal experiential state of a subject. Others may witness a person enduring a mystical episode, but they do not share the experience and are not aware of its content unless conveyed to them by the subject. Even when two people have mystical perceptions together at the same time and place, each has a private experience. Neither experience is shared. It is in this first sense that a mystical experience is indeed private. Let us call this 'psychological privacy'.

In another sense of 'private', some mystical experiences are not private at all. Mystics have shared their experiences with others, reporting their experiences and relating what occurred in having them. In this sense, these mystical perceptions have not remained private. They have become public. Let us say that mystical experiences enjoy 'sociological privacy', then, when subjects keep it to themselves, or when having negligible social or political meaning. Sociologically, private experiences remain in the 'private realm'.

Now Jantzen has done an outstanding job of showing that mystical experiences sometimes, at least, are anything but private, if sociological privacy is in question. It would be a gross mistake to believe that mystical experiences are all or generally private in the sociological sense. Mystics proclaim their experiences to others, and mystical episodes or enduring states sometimes serve as centers from which power and prestige ensue. They have served also as reason for the repression of mystics. Indeed, we have seen in the previous chapter how an attempted explanation of theistic mystical experiences by Evan Fales builds on the political and social power potentials of mystical experiences. So every student of mysticism should be aware of mysticism's sociological publicity and meaning.

However, this does not imply that mystical experience is not private in the psychological sense of privacy. Indeed, such experiences are psychologically private. Epistemological inquiries into mystical experiences relate to them in the latter sense of 'privacy', without prejudicing the issue of their sociological privacy. Hence, my focusing on such private experiences, in my sense, should not be taken as suggesting or agreeing implicitly to an attempt to relegate women to a private sociological domain.

Another way of putting this point would be to distinguish mystical experience from the entire phenomenon of mysticism. While a mystical experience is indeed private to the person having the experience, 'mysticism' encompasses far more than the private. Mysticism encompasses psychologically private mystical experiences, as well as mystical philosophy, literature, art, schools and institutions, and social and political movements. Dealing with mystical *experience* as private does not imply thinking of mysticism as private. Neither does studying mystical experience preclude studying these other dimensions of mysticism.

Finally, Jantzen sometimes writes as though male philosophers were guilty simply for failing, in their work, to engage in topics that would advance social justice and the alleviation of oppression. As we have seen, at one point she says that, 'The net result, whatever the intention of the authors and compilers, is the reinforcement of the societal status quo, as intellectual and religious energy is poured into an exploration of private religiosity rather than into social and political action for change' (1995, p. 21). So maybe the root problem for Jantzen is that energy is being put into topics that fail to advance the cause of the oppressed.

Note that this critique of philosophers of mysticism spreads far beyond its stated mark. It applies equally to anyone whose professional 'energies' are 'poured into' endeavors not connected to social and political change. Jantzen's rebuke would apply to logicians, many epistemologists, many historians of philosophy and philosophers of language. It would also apply to theoretical mathematicians, most physicists, many historians, linguists, many scholars of literature, and more. It would also apply to all non-academics going about making a living in anything not connected to promoting social justice. It would tar all of these not because of some repressive intent or content in their work, but purely because of the nature of their disciplines or occupations in relation to working for social justice. This offensive against variegated human endeavor in the name of an all-encompassing occupation with social activism may be understandable, given the extent of the social injustices Jantzen wishes us to oppose, but is hardly defensible. Jantzen, furthermore, provides insufficient reason to think philosophers are obligated more than anyone else to set aside their interests and occupations for exclusive dedication to social activism.

I conclude that the task of evaluating the evidential value of mystical experiences, theistic mystical experiences among them, need not be considered harmful to women or otherwise morally reprehensible. I add that nevertheless it is important for philosophers of mysticism to be well aware of the problems of injustice involved in their topic. My inclusion of this topic in my study has been motivated, in part, by the desire to do so. We can thank Grace Jantzen and other feminist philosophers for helping us to understand this.

The Epistemological Critique

My enterprise is entrenched in a circle of concepts that some feminists believe must be restructured or replaced. Implicated here are such concepts as 'experience', 'evidence', 'justification' and 'rationality'. These concepts, this feminist claim goes, are androcentric constructions (see Alcoff and Potter, 1993; Code, 1991; and Harding, 1991). Hence, an uncritical account of experience and evidence would beg the question of male privilege.

On the epistemological critique, the use of the above concepts is infected by a bogus conception of neutrality and objectivity. A neutral or objective standpoint pretends to provide judgments free of personal, class and gender interests. However, in reality what has passed for 'objectivity' reflects nothing else than the judgments of upper middle-class white Western males, in what Sandra Harding calls 'weak objectivity' (Harding, 1993). Accounts centering on male perspectives are weakly objective. In wrongly supposing they have entered a neutral space, upper middle-class white Western males have failed to be conscious of the implicit gendered and class attitudes and beliefs they carry with them unawares into the 'neutral' space. So what has seemed to them reasonable, from their unnoticed particular standpoint, has been jacked-up to the heights of objectivity. Feminists, in turn, have the task of raising awareness to uncover the implicit attitudes and beliefs imposed on a supposedly neutral standpoint.

If I uncritically approached the epistemology of mystical experiences of God without minding the feminist critique of the fundamental conceptual framework that shapes my account of experience, I would merely reassert the androcentric point of view.

We should not misinterpret this feminist critique. In acknowledging that concepts like 'experience', 'rationality' and 'evidence' are social constructions, feminist philosophers (for the most part) do not mean to deny that a social construction can have reference to an objective reality. Therefore, they would not disagree with the following.

Consider the concept of a 'chair'. This concept is a social construction. The conceptual demarcation between chairs and non-chairs are rather arbitrarily fixed according to various needs and expectations. At least some non-chairs could have been considered chairs, and may one day be so considered, if we were interested in moving the demarcation between chairs and non-chairs. It hardly follows, however, that chairs are nothing more than a social construction. Chairs, after all, are physical objects with plenty of properties of their own on their own. A native of a deep jungle who had never seen a chair and with no concept of chairs would experience the same resistance if she tried to walk through a jungle space where a chair was placed, as would a scientist walking through her experimental laboratory who bumped into a chair on her way. Chairs are not only social constructs.

What feminist philosophers are concerned to argue is, rather, that the construction put upon reality often displays an androcentric bias. Return to the concepts of 'experience', 'rationality' and 'evidence'. Feminist thought renders an important service by unmasking the sometimes subtle, unnoticed constructions put on these notions in our daily life – the question: 'Whose experience, rationality and evidence?' is always appropriate. We must ever be on guard for insidious components grafted on to the notion of 'experience' in its social construction. We must be sensitive to the question, 'Whose experience counts as evidence?', making sure we do not identify 'evidence' with what one sector of humankind recognizes. Here, I would recommend a good dose of 'standpoint epistemology', with its notion of 'strong objectivity', as a welcome corrective to a too narrow construal of 'experience' and of 'evidence'. Roughly, strong objectivity requires us to think our claims from the perspective of others and to see our lives from the other's position.[1] Construed realistically, and not relativistically, thinking from a multiple of standpoints helps us to come closer to the objective truth. We are forced to an awareness of the biases attached to each limited perspective, advancing toward a widening appreciation of the reality we experience.

When dealing with mystical experience of God, in particular, philosophers should be open to the richness of content and texture of women's experiences and interpretations thereof. What I have called earlier in this work 'mystical traditions' may have been formed in relative neglect of women's mystical experiences, though there are some clear exceptions, and should be enriched and reshaped in light of new research. This will no doubt have an affect on what sorts of perceptual contents should be considered indications of a direct experience of God.

At the same time, we cannot get away from the fact that our experiences do count as evidence in favor of and against propositions we entertain. We know, for example, of the problem of androcentric constructions by way of experience. We know by experience that white male bias infects the concept of 'objectivity', and that therefore we should not take white males' word for it if we really want to be objective. We know from experience that women suffer from patriarchal construals. And so on. If such claims are not to reflect simply a new, feminist, bias, they will appeal to experience as their evidence. If some feminists believe the objectionable concepts to be too infected by patriarchal biases to be of use any longer, we could coin new terms or qualify old ones, as in 'weak' and 'strong' objectivity.

Evidence

Sometimes, feminists seem to be bothered by talk about 'evidence', thinking male epistemologists want to require having evidence before being 'allowed' to 'believe' something, belief taken to mean assent to a lone proposition.[2] Making such a requirement for the ethics of belief, however, could entail the imposition of a particular concept of 'rationality' and 'belief' that feminists challenge. The requirement of evidence in rationally warranting a belief turns questions related to how we should live into questions about what discrete 'beliefs' are supported by what evidence 'out there' in the world. In so doing, we neglect the complex interrelationships of beliefs and ignore the relevance of ethical and political issues to the debate. If this feminist critique is successful, it applies especially to any attempt to reduce questions about God to ones about 'evidence' and 'belief', rather than about what is at stake in the God questions in the first place. Those questions touch deeply on how we see the world, and ourselves, and influence strongly our understanding of how to contribute to the flourishing of human values. On this epistemological critique, questions about God, such as God's existence and God's appearing to people in mystical experiences, are clear paradigms of questions requiring an approach broader than an evidentialist one to discrete 'beliefs'.

In response, I point out that some philosophers who have written extensively about the rationality of religious belief and the evidence for it have also declared that evidence was not needed for warranted belief. Most famously, Alvin Plantinga has argued for the 'proper basicality' of believing, for example, that God loves me (Plantinga, 1979 and 1981). I have endorsed the view that in order to be justified in accepting a belief as true one need not be in possession of good evidence for that belief. I have argued that some beliefs, including some religious beliefs, could be what I call 'rock-bottom' beliefs, not based on any evidence (Gellman, 1993). In addition, through reading feminist literature, I have come to appreciate the possibility of thinking in terms other than 'objective' 'evidence' for a 'belief', to describe our cognitive postures in the world. So I do not endorse thinking that evidence is essential for our cognitive postures.

Nonetheless, questions of evidence for discrete beliefs will not go away. We are constantly forming discrete beliefs based on evidence. When I look at my watch and come to believe it is 4:00, I am forming a discrete belief because of visual evidence, and I form the discrete belief that the cat is sitting alongside my leg based on various tactile and olfactory evidences. Naturally, each of these beliefs is embedded in a complex of other attitudes, beliefs and behaviors, and neither belief exists in isolation from the rest. That does not change the basic point, though, that we regularly form discrete beliefs on pieces of evidence. There is no avoiding doing so. Although the question of God involves much more than a discrete belief that God exists or that God appears to humans, I submit that seeking evidence for God-questions is meaningful and relevant to the wider perspectives on our cognitive stances in the world.

The Argument from Perception presents an evidential argument for thinking God genuinely appears in mystical experiences. This argument can well be supplemented by other, non-evidential arguments. In addition, any attempt to deny that God is ever mystically perceived will have to consider the evidence supporting the opposite conclusion. By the end of the day, therefore, the evidential case for genuine God-perceptions must be addressed, even if we do this within a wider and richer context.

The Theological Critique

The theological critique from the direction of feminist thought takes issue
with the 'classical' concept of God assumed, implicitly or explicitly, in
standard discussions of mystical experience by male philosophers. Since I
too have countenanced the classical concept of God, along with what I have
called the 'generic' concept, the feminist critique sticks to me too.[3] The
classical concept of God is objectionable because, it is claimed, it represents
male desire, to the exclusion of female desire. Consequently, male philosophers think of what mystical experiences disclose in terms that only men
would recognize. In the process, philosophers marginalize women and wom-
en's theological (or 'thealogical') preferences.

Although God, the Hebrew Bible says, created man in his own image,
feminist theologians and philosophers of religion tend to see this the other
way around: man has created God in his own image, and the results have
caused suffering for women. Traditionally, on the feminist critique, the
concept of God tended to reflect the most cherished values and self-
perceptions principally of advantaged, white males who saw themselves at
the apex of human hierarchical existence, with women subjugated to them.
Nancy Frankenberry puts the critique as follows (Frankenberry, 1998,
p. 177):

> Whether taken as real or unreal, inferred validly or invalidly, experienced di-
> rectly or projected illusorily, the divine identity in classical theism has been
> unmistakably male. More problematically, the supreme, ruling, judging, as well
> as loving, male God envisioned as a single, absolute subject and named Father
> has been conceived as standing in a relation of hierarchical domination to the
> world. In ways both implicit and explicit, this has tended in turn to justify
> various social and political structures of patriarchy that exalt solitary human
> patriarchs at the head of pyramids of power. Drawn almost exclusively from the
> world of ruling-class men, traditional theistic concepts and images have func-
> tioned effectively to legitimate social and intellectual structures that grant a
> theomorphic character to men who rule but that relegate women, children, and
> other men to marginalized and subordinated areas.

Thus, God represents an idealized, powerful male, at the head of a hierarchy
of beings subject to his word and command. The God of tradition, according
to this, is a social construct that has marginalized women and their point of
view, and has under-pinned patriarchal oppression of women. Indeed, according to some feminists, monotheism was a major creator of patriarchal
oppression (Ochshorn, 1981).

The God of tradition is supposed to be eternal, free, all-powerful, all
knowing, perfectly good, and omnipresent, whose will is perfectly realized.
Feminists charge that 'on the ground' men have favored God's freedom,
power and control as the divine traits worth emulating. God exercises
unimpeded control over everything, everywhere, enjoying massive dominat-

ing power over others. This is a man's dream for himself, as an autonomous, all-powerful being, who dominates by simple fiat.[4] The key concept for understanding God, therefore, is 'power-over', rather than the humanly enabling concept of 'power-to' (see Allen, 1998). As a result, men's relationship to God reflects a hierarchical system of subordination and superordination, a hierarchy from God to men, and then from men to women.

The Critique of 'Mystical Experience'

The traditional male construction of God, the feminist critique continues, has informed the way men philosophers think of mystical experience. Melissa Raphael puts the idea as follows: 'Feminist criticism argues that religious experience is conditioned from the outset by patriarchal conceptualizations of ultimate value and by sex-role differentiation in the practice of religion' (Raphael, 1994, p. 513).

Typically, men understand mystical experience as a human subject encountering a being wholly distinct distant, and overpowering. A paradigm of this approach is in the highly influential writings of Rudolf Otto concerning the experience of the 'numinous', for Otto the root experience of the divine.

The experience of the numinous is of an uncanny reality, 'wholly other' than the subject. This reality appears as a *'mysterium tremendum et fascinans'*, unfathomable, overpowering, and engendering a sense of dreaded fascination. The mystic realizes in his mystical states that he is a 'creature', 'submerged and overwhelmed by its own nothingness in contrast to that which is supreme above all creatures' (Otto, 1957, p. 10). Otto's subject is thus duly overwhelmed by the majestic *tremendum* before which he bows in terror.

This portrayal, while claiming to capture a universal human response to the divine numinous presence, reflects for feminists nothing other than a biased, masculine construction upon mystical experience. Melissa Raphael gives voice to a feminist rejection of this construction: 'The concepts and language [Otto] used to evoke, categorize, and value numinous experience reveal that this kind of experience ... is mediated and constituted by the androcentrism of Otto's world view and by that of the history of religions itself' (Raphael, 1994, pp. 512–13). The great influence upon subsequent thinkers of Otto's idea of numinous experience reinforces Raphael's charge of masculine bias in the study of mystical experience.

A feminist paradigm of mystical experience would look quite different from Otto's. For example, many feminists would deny a dichotomy between the holy and the creaturely that makes Otto's analysis possible (see Goldenberg, 1979, and Daly, 1991). Feminist theology would likely stress the immanent nature of the 'object' of mystical experience, and bring to prominence women's experience of sacrality in the very embodiment denigrated by androcentric attitudes to lowly 'flesh'.

Raphael cites the example of Monica Sjoo, a 'Goddess feminist', to illuminate a feminist way with mystical experience. Sjoo described her experience at Silbury mound in these terms (quoted in Raphael, 1994, p. 522):

> I look at Her mound ... so exposed ... like veins on a breast streaking Her sides ... again overwhelmed by tears and sorrow. I now understand what Mother Earth means ... something so enormous, powerful ... also so painful in my own woman's body which is like Hers ... violent but gentle ... powerful but vulnerable.

Realists and Non-realists

On grounds such as these, feminist theologians and philosophers of religion endorse the re-configuring of the concept of God, and of mystical experience of God, to eliminate the age-old male bias. These same thinkers part company, however, on how they perceive their enterprise. Some are theological non-realists, maintaining that 'God' does not refer to any object or reality. Others are theological realists, though they might differ as to the reference of 'God'.

Pamela Anderson has developed a non-realist concept of God. Anderson's approach is neo-Kantian, according to which the concept of God is taken to be a 'regulative' concept. Anderson writes that (Anderson, 1998, p. 229):

> following Kant, especially in the light of Horkheimer, it is possible to agree that according to the philosophical terms set out in previous chapters, the existence of a god or goddess could mean an ideal existence in the sense of the projection of a goal for which one strives ... This ideal is known to exist in a practical sense as it functions in thinking and living.

Anderson calls this a 'regulative' sense of 'exist', and is careful to distinguish such an ideal from a mere 'fiction', which cannot serve as a 'practical ideal or regulative principle' (p. 229). In addition, 'projection of a goal' in the above quotation is not to be confused with psychological projection of the sort about which Feuerbach wrote.[5]

Anderson maintains, though, that the God-concept has done more than merely express and guide our most cherished values and self-conceptions. It has created an illusion, in constituting idealized knowledge of man and his relationship to the divine. Similar to Kant's thought that practical reason required the positing of God to reinforce morality, Anderson suggests that the concept of the divine should be reconfigured to function to focus and guide our desire for justice and love. The divine, then, would not be a personal being, although it could represent a practical ideal to guide action toward the highest good. Anderson's refiguration of the divine (or 'God') fashions a non-realist conception of God (or 'God').

Other feminists are realists about God. Daphne Hampson is this sort of theological realist. Hampson rejects the Christian tradition because of its conception of God, writing: 'Is He, one wonders, the reflection of what has been many a man's wildest dreams?' (Hampson, 1990, p. 151; see also Hampson, 1996). Yet Hampson supports a realist reconfiguration of the God-concept. Unlike Anderson, Hampson employs realist terms in relation to God and so proclaims: 'I am not, then, saying that God is a human projection. I believe the word God to refer, and that moreover some theologies may better fit what we may believe to be the case than others' (p. 150), and (p. 169):

> [The word 'God'] is not simply a construct in language; however profoundly our conceptualization of God be shaped by the linguistic and cultural tradition in which we belong. Nor is using religious language for me simply a way of naming the world, a way of affirming (for example) that I will have faith that there is an underlying goodness.

Hampson is a theological realist because she believes that God is an 'object' of human experience and because she wants to account for the efficacy of prayer, especially when one prays for others (pp. 169ff.).[6] When it comes to conceptualizing God, Hampson recognizes the crucial significance of ethical considerations. A conceptualization sensitive to feminist concerns is ethically superior to others, for her (p. 150). So Hampson's concept of God, although realist about God, possesses a clear, regulative component.

Whether realist or non-realist, feminist theologians and philosophers of religion are out to undo the traditional, classical concept of God.

Peter Byrne on Omnipotence

Some have contended against the feminist project of reconfiguring God. In an important response to feminist theology, Peter Byrne has provided a carefully argued rejoinder to a feminist critique of divine power that can be generalized to other attributes (Byrne, 1995). Byrne reminds us that, 'whatever God's power is, it is one with his goodness, mercy, love, life, knowledge, etc.' (p. 149). Given these other metaphysically essential properties of God, God cannot do wrong. Since domineering power is bad, says Byrne, 'it is simply not within the power of God to evince it' (p. 152). Byrne goes on to elucidate the traditional notion of divine power, showing that it is devoid of elements objectionable to feminists. Byrne concludes that the classic idea of God does not lead to the abuses feminists have uncovered in the history of religions.

Some would wish to reply to Byrne as Mary Daly has written in a related context: 'This kind of defense is understandable but it leaves a basic question unanswered: if the symbol *can* be "used" that way and in fact has a long history of being "used" that way, isn't this an indication of some inherent deficiency in the symbol itself?' (Daly, 1973, p. 72). Byrne is ready with a response to this sort of objection: 'The fact that some have used the notion of a true source of final authority in the universe to justify what are in fact

illegitimate uses of power does not in itself show that this notion is mis-
guided' (1995, p. 162). And 'What the feminist critique must make us
believe is that there is an inevitable, or at least, very powerful, impulse in
the idea of sovereign deity which serves to make us accept as right and
unquestionable any established claims to power in the world' (p. 163).
Byrne adds that feminists have so far failed to establish what they must
make 'us' believe.

Now I am inclined to agree with Byrne that on the conceptual level the
classic idea of God need not be responsible for androcentric abuses in
theistic religions. Nevertheless, historically, on the ground, theistic religions, officially, or in the everyday life of their adherents, have displayed
serious injustices toward women. That these injustices have been given the
mantle of holiness and inviolability has made them that more powerful. To
morally justify a revision of the traditional concept of God, therefore, it is
not necessary to demonstrate that the very idea of God somehow inevitably
produces such evil results. It might suffice to show that human beings are
such that in traditional theistic frameworks sociological and psychological
forces have come into play that brought such evils to be.

Then too, Byrne's response underestimates the extent of the biases
against women in the history of theistic religions, that may be due at least
in part to notions of hierarchal domination of men over women, mirroring
the hierarchal power of God over his dominion. The biases have been far-
reaching and systematic over history, notwithstanding minority voices to
the contrary in theological traditions. It is not simply, as Byrne says, that
'some' have abused power under the influence of hierarchical conceptions.
Therefore, while Byrne's reply is correct as far as it goes, it may not go far
enough.

Furthermore, some feminists, at least, will say that, aside from the practical effects on women, women simply cannot identify with the patriarchal
God of history. An autonomous, powerful, transcendent being just doesn't
speak to them. The concept of God must be revised so that women can
recognize themselves in their religious practice. So even were we to eliminate androcentric abuses, there would still be a good reason to press for a
revised or wholly new understanding of God.

On Reconfiguring the Concept of God

Various strands of feminism propose different strategies for redoing the
concept of God. Some propose mixing masculine and feminine pronouns
and characteristics when speaking of God to make God user friendly for
both men and women. This proposal goes well, perhaps, with a 'libertarian'
form of feminism that seeks to overcome gender differences between males
and females.[7] Other sorts of feminists substitute a Goddess for God, replacing a male God with a feminine one. Sometimes this move is made within
traditional religion (as in Gross, 1983). Others, such as Anderson, as we

have seen, propose a concept of God regulating desires for justice and human flourishing.

These proposals, despite wide differences between them, share the conviction that somehow God is to reflect one's highest values and aspirations. Consequently, the religious life consists of our striving to be 'God-like', trying to embody God-like features or values in our own lives. The assumption is that our concept of God should express what we value in ourselves, or how we see our ideal selves. In this way, the concept of God is driven by a religious orientation of 'imitating' God. The feminist critique of traditional religion is that its God is a masculine projection of what men would wish to be like. Feminist proposals retain this basic attitude of *imitatio dei* only wishing to project a feminist, or neutral, ideal rather than a masculine one.

The extent to which *imitatio dei* figures axiomatically in feminist thought is attested to by the theme to be found there of 'becoming divine'. Luce Irigary is a good example of this approach when she writes, 'God forces us to do nothing except *become*. The only task, the obligation laid upon us is: to become divine men and women, to become perfectly, to refuse to allow parts of ourselves to shrivel and die that have the potential for growth and fulfillment' (Irigary, 1993, pp. 68–9). Likewise, in her work *Becoming Divine*, Grace Jantzen centers on 'becoming divine' through 'natality', or the continued coming to birth of the self.

In this respect, feminist theology and philosophy of religion remain quite traditional in their religious outlook. They go along with the *imitatio dei* idea, replacing a supposedly masculine ideal with an acceptable one. However the oppression feminists associate with the classical concept of God is a result of the combination of the concept and the *imitatio dei* ideal together. Were men not convinced of their having to be like God, presumably the power of the classical God-concept to make mischief would be downgraded or eliminated. By retaining the idea of becoming divine, feminist thinkers force a rejection of the classical conception of God in favor of more congenial constructions.

I propose a different route toward undoing patriarchal abuses of the concept of God. Rather than retaining the doctrine of *imitatio dei* and disowning the classical concept of God, I propose rethinking the concept of imitating God while retaining the classical God-concept. I propose this not as a protective strategy for the classical God concept but, as we will see, in the name of an ethically acceptable theology. My proposal comes in two versions. The first, more moderate, version means to remain within the tradition of imitation of God while severely restricting its application. This proposal will thus appeal to religious traditionalists. The second, more radical version, de-emphasizes *imitatio dei* altogether. While retaining an affinity to some strands of traditional religious thought, this version will appeal to those more prepared to depart from traditional doctrines and texts.

A Restricted Doctrine of *Imitatio Dei*

My first version of a rethinking of the *imitatio dei* doctrine is a construction broadly based on Moses Maimonides' treatment of the subject, in his *Guide of the Perplexed* and *Mishneh Torah*.[8] I will show how a creative development of Maimonides can help us advance toward eliminating what is objectionable about the notion of our imitating God.[9]

Maimonides' doctrine of *imitatio dei* can be summarized as follows:[10]

1   Every positive statement of the form: 'God is P' is false, where 'P' is any non-relational descriptive predicate or term we can understand. So, for example, 'God is wise' is false. Hence, we can make true negative statements about God, all of which are of the form: 'It is not the case that God is P' where 'P' is any non-relational descriptive predicate or term we can understand. So we can truly say 'God is not wise', without implying that God is ignorant (since 'God is ignorant' too is a false, positive statement). The negative statements record God's 'negative attributes' (see *Guide of the Perplexed*, 1963, Part 1, Chapters 58–60).

2   We can make true statements about God's actions, of the form 'God brings about (or causes) state of affairs, S'. These statements record God's 'attributes of action'.

3   Any religiously endorsed statement that describes God acting from a passion or emotion, such as 'God acted angrily toward the Israelites' is to be analyzed into this form: 'God brings about (or causes) some state of affairs such that ordinarily were *we* to act so as to bring about such a state of affairs, we would be doing so from that emotion or passion.' In providing this analysis, we avoid ascribing emotions or passions to God (see Part 1, Chapter 54).

4   The statements in (1), (2) and (3) are all the true statements we can make about God, except for non-descriptive, evaluative statements, such as: 'God possesses supreme value' or 'God is the supreme being', and certain relational statements (Part 1, Chapter 35 and 54).[11]

5   Any religiously endorsed statement that attributes to God a *character trait*, such as being merciful or being gracious, as opposed to action statements, such as 'acts mercifully' or 'acts graciously', is false of God (taking 'acts' as a relational predicate). This follows from clause (1). Such statements have a purely didactic/regulative purpose: they (pretend to) ascribe such character traits to God as a way of telling us that we should cultivate and strive to exemplify those traits (Part 1, Chapter 54).

6   At this point there are two versions in Maimonides' writings.

Version A   In *Mishneh Torah*, the imitation of God is exhausted by character-traits ascribed to God in the Hebrew Bible, as per (5), and does not include statements of the kind in (1)–(3). Maimonides writes there (*Mishneh Torah, Laws of Character-Traits*, Chapter 1, Law 6, my translation):

> Just as He is called 'compassionate', so shall you be compassionate; just as He is called 'merciful', so shall you be merciful; just as He is called 'holy', so shall you be holy. And in this way the prophets called God with all these names: 'slow to anger' and 'full of kindness', 'righteous' and 'honest', 'faithful', 'valiant' and 'strong', and such, to make known that these are good and straight ways and that a person should train himself according to them and imitate Him as much as possible.[12]

There are three terms here that beg elucidation: 'holy' (*kadosh*)', 'valiant' (*gibor*) and 'strong' (*hazak*). Let's look at each of these in turn.

Holy: The literal meaning of the Hebrew word *kadosh* is 'separated from' or 'set aside'. Based on what Maimonides writes elsewhere, 'holiness' has to do with keeping a proper distance from an attachment to the flesh, especially with regard to sexual activity (*Mishneh Torah*, Laws of Character-Traits, Chapter 2, Law 4, and Chapter 5, Law 4). Just as God is distant from the flesh, so must we be, to the extent possible for 'flesh and blood'.

This notion will not pass a feminist critique that sees the defamation of the body and the physical as a weapon men have wielded against women. In addition, in a discussion of Jewish feminism and separation, Drorah Setel spoke for some feminists when she decried the 'separational perspectives' of Judaism and the Bible that are 'expressed in misogynist metaphors' (Setel, 1986, p. 115).[13] Setel rejects separation in favor of relationship. Referring to separation as a governing conception, she says that 'As a Jewish feminist I think my present task is to speak no longer in that obsolete mode' (p. 118).

In that same discussion, Marcia Falk acknowledged that separation has invariably led to hierarchical scaffolding, including causing women to be 'separated from' men in a hierarchical way (Falk, 1986, p. 121). Unlike Setel, though, Falk has argued for retaining the separation motif in a way that was not hierarchal (Falk, 1986 and 1996, pp. 43–50 and 487–93; see also Rita Gross's contribution to this symposium, in Gross, 1986).

In the light of these potential difficulties, it might be good to be able to supply an alternative understanding in which holiness is not equivalent to anti-body or to separation in any sinister sense. In the Hebrew Bible, 'holiness' connotes not only 'separation from', but also being dedicated to or set aside for God. So we could say that God is 'holy' in the sense of being dedicated to God's purposes. God does not stray from God's purposes. We, too, should be 'holy', then, by dedicating our lives to God's purposes. This need not be taken with a radically heteronymous meaning, necessarily implying a denial of one's own purposes. It could be that we live God's purposes best when we live our own deepest selves. The holiness of following our deepest selves might turn out to be the very same holiness of following God's purposes.

Valiant: In the Bible it says that God is a 'man of war', but Maimonides did not wish to teach that we should be 'valiant' in the sense of warlike. Most likely he was thinking of the rabbinical dictum: 'Who is valiant? The one who conquers the evil inclination.' Accordingly, Maimonides writes elsewhere of the person who is 'valiant' with regard to restraint in responding to insults, and successful in overcoming unseemly personal desires (*Mishneh Torah*, Laws of Character-Traits, Chapter 2, Law 3, and Chapter 4, Law 10). So our imitation of God's 'valor' consists in our applying ourselves to the sublimation of our own undesirable impulses.

Strong: In the Hebrew Bible God is referred to as 'strong' (*hazak*) as in Jeremiah 50:34 because God is a strong redeemer, who fights the enemies of Israel. And God is said to take the people of Israel out of Egypt with a 'strong hand'. Maimonides did not mean to teach we should be fighting our enemies in order to be as God-like as possible. I imagine he means we should be 'strong' in the sense in which God calls upon various biblical characters to be strong (*hazak*), namely they should be steadfast and persevere. So, for Maimonides we are to imitate God by being steadfast in our tasks and in our opposition to evil.

Version B   That is the first version of this part of Maimonides' doctrine. As opposed to this *Mishneh Torah* version of the imitation doctrine, in his *Guide for the Perplexed*, Maimonides holds that the imitation of God is limited to the attributes ascribed to God in Exodus 34: 6–7 (*Guide*, 1963, Part 1, Chapter 54). The verses there read as follows:

> The Lord passed before him and the Lord proclaimed: The Lord is a God who is compassionate and gracious, slow to anger, steadfast in kindness, extending kindness to the thousandth generation, forgiving iniquity, transgression, and sin; remitting punishment, yet [in some circumstances] He does not remit sin, but visits the iniquity of fathers upon children and children's children, upon the third and fourth generations.[14]

In Maimonides' explication of these verses, all attributes, save one, involve attributes of charity, such as kindness, mercy, and patience. The one exception is God's punishing wrongdoing. Maimonides suggests that the latter be invoked only rarely, and that the charitable attributes should dominate our behavior.[15]

It turns out that each of the attributes included in the doctrine of *imitatio dei* in the *Guide* is either the name of a character trait or subsumable under one. So, in this respect, the *Guide* doctrine differs little from the one in *Mishneh Torah*. In other respects, there are important differences between the doctrine as it appears in these two sources, but these differences are not germane to the present discussion.[16] So in what follows I will refer to the *Mishneh Torah* doctrine simply as 'Maimonides' doctrine'.

What the Doctrine Excludes

Now let's see what Maimonides' doctrine excludes from the imitation of God. While there are biblical passages in which God is presented as acting vengefully or angrily, these do not describe God as possessing the *character trait* of being an 'avenger' or as it were an 'angerer', a person of anger. Therefore for Maimonides these descriptions are not candidates for the doctrine of *imitatio dei*. We are not called on to imitate God's 'angry' or 'vengeful' acts. Instead, such verses are to be analyzed as in (3) above, as saying that God acts in ways that are such that if *we* were to act in those ways ordinarily we would do so from anger or vengeance. God does not act from such motives or emotions. Neither are we to do so.

Pains were taken in rabbinical literature, too, to exclude attributes such as jealousy and vengeance from the imitation motif, and emphasize charity, as in the following teaching (Babylonian Talmud, Tractate Sotah 14a):

> Rabbi Hama son of Rabbi Hanina said: What does it mean 'You shall follow after the Lord your God (Deuteronomy, **13**:4)?' Is it possible for a person to follow the divine presence [*shechinah*]? It is stated 'for the Lord your God is a consuming fire (Deuteronomy 4:24)'! However, [the verse] means to follow after the characteristics of the Holy One Blessed be He. Just as He clothes the naked ... so shall you clothe the naked; [just as] God visited the sick ... so shall you visit the sick; [just as] God consoles mourners ... so shall you console mourners; [just as] God buried the dead, so you shall bury the dead.[17]

Most pointedly, Maimonides' doctrine excludes terms that ascribe to God an office, function, or relationship, since these are not names for character traits. In particular, Maimonides' doctrine excludes the terms: 'king', 'ruler', 'lord' and 'father' from the domain of imitation. 'King', for example, does not denote a character trait, but an office or position. I suggest that Maimonides would apply to the statement that God is (a) king an analysis comparable to that given in clause (2) to action-statements. In addition, Maimonides' doctrine excludes being a 'supremely valuable being', from the realm of imitation of God, since the doctrine is limited to descriptions in terms of character traits only, and then only to ones occurring in the Bible.

A neo-Maimonidean version of *imitatio dei* has much that is congenial to feminist thought:

1   Although Maimonides is not a non-realist all the way up, his doctrine bears affinities to a non-realist construal of the God-concept. He shares with that construal the thought that the positive descriptive content of our God-concept should be reconfigured as a practical ideal to guide

action toward the good. We could call this a 'regulative' view (regarding the positive, descriptive content, at least) of the God-concept,
although this would not be equivalent to the rather technical Kantian
sense of 'regulative'. We have also seen that Hampson's realist theology
gives a significant place to ethical regulative considerations in working
out the concept of God, which goes well with the neo-Maimonidean
scheme.

2   The Maimonidean attributes of God we are to imitate should be quite
     welcome from a feminist point of view, realist and non-realist alike.

3   Being like God by being like a king, father, lord or master, is no part of
     Maimonides' doctrine. The sheer exercise of power and domination of
     others is no part of the regulative concept of God, either for Maimonides
     or for the feminists. Imitating God for Maimonides' doctrine would not
     be a way of justifying patriarchy or otherwise imposing male subjuga-
     tion of women.

4   Maimonides' doctrine precludes imitating God as 'creator'. Carol Delaney
     has contended that the imitation of God has informed the notion of God
     as 'creator'. It was men, she claims, not women, who were considered
     the creators par excellence (Delaney, 1998, Part Two). Thus, according
     to Delaney there was set in place an insidious equation: just as God
     creates by power-over, so men act creatively by exercising their power-
     over. A clear example of this kind of application of the imitation of God
     is implied in the following commentary from the Jewish tradition about
     being in 'the image of God': 'Man is made in the image of God. So
     when he finds himself perfect in himself, without diverging from God's
     way, his power is very great, and he will rule over all, even over the
     heavenly hosts.'[18] Clearly, the author thinks of the image of God and the
     consequent being 'like' God in terms of power-over, and this, feminists
     have taught, has been deleterious for women. Maimonides' version of
     imitatio dei precludes such an application.

In sum, Maimonides' understanding of the imitation of God would have
us start with an abstract evaluative concept of God as something like: 'God
possesses supreme value.' When considering positive descriptive predications
of God, the imitation of God becomes only a device for guiding our moral
lives, since no such predications are true of God. Ontologically speaking,
when we 'imitate' God by being kind, for example, our imitation does not
consist in our being kind as God is, but in our becoming intrinsically
worthy, as God is. This is the irreducible axiological component of *imitatio
dei* for Maimonides. The doctrine comes down to this: become an intrinsically worthy person, just as God is intrinsically valuable.

To summarize, the first rethinking of the idea of our imitating God would
stress the severe restriction upon the imitation motif, disqualifying all but
the attributes of charity, and the relatively rare imitation of punishing behavior.
Excluded as well would be any hierarchal imitation of God's lordship or

mastership. Thus do we weaken the harmful potential of abuses of the classical concept of God. Or so it would seem.

A Critique of the First Proposal

So far, I have been presenting a more traditional way of attempting to right the injustices resulting from a generalized conception of imitation of God. However, some feminist theologians and philosophers of religion may meet with this traditional tack with less than enthusiasm. The reason is that there can be a great difference, after all, between arid, abstract, religious and theological doctrines, and the way those doctrines function in practice. So it is not enough that an abstract theological doctrine be acceptable, it must also have a good chance to remain so in practice.

Specifically, the traditional approach I just outlined might lack the power to translate itself into action, because overly optimistic about the practicality of limiting the imitation of God to selected personal characteristics. In historical monotheism, the idea of our making ourselves like God has manifested far wider implications than the restricted doctrine allows, including those feminists point out as leading to serious injustice. If we allow even a restricted doctrine of imitation while retaining a classical concept of God, we may implicitly allow imitation to spill over beyond its set boundaries. This is especially so, it might be supposed, with the lurking in the background of biblical images of God that feminists would see as encouraging the imitation overspill.

In light of this critique, the second proposal concerning the imitation of God departs from traditional ideas in order to de-emphasize the imitation theme entirely. For the remainder of this chapter I will present this more radical strategy for meeting the feminist critique of historical monotheism.

Non-imitative Theology

The second proposal stresses that we should not be guided by the desire to be like God.[19] This approach contrasts sharply with Feuerbach who maintained (at least at one point in his life) that God was a human projection, away from and beyond humankind, embodying the fullest expression of just those characteristics we most cherish in ourselves.[20] In Feuerbach's eyes, this projection represented a failure of nerve, an alienation of humans from themselves, since they thereby denied their own possession of their most valued characteristics. Instead, they displaced these attributes on to a transcendent God. Feuerbach contended that religion would fade from human culture to the extent that humanity became reconciled with itself, then taking on the responsibility and challenge of the greatness of humankind. Then the projection of human attributes would cease, and God would disappear.

On the second proposal, to the contrary, we should consider the 'divine attributes' of God to be forever beyond human attainment. When human beings become reconciled with themselves, they will realize this and will not wish to be like God. On this theological conception, divine attributes are forever and in principle beyond our ability to embody in ourselves. All of perfection is projected beyond us outward, to an unreachable place. God, then, is not a model for us. God is a warning to us. God is a warning that might be summed up in these words written by Aldous Huxley in *Point Counterpoint*: 'When we try to make ourselves more than human, we make ourselves less than human.' We can make ourselves less than human by striving to be God-like. We can make ourselves less than human by modeling ourselves on that which is more than human, and thus frustrating our endeavors and leaving our human possibilities underdeveloped. On this idea, God is to be worshipped, but not imitated.

An easy way of carrying out this non-imitative theology would be to pick up on a traditional idea that God is 'unknowable' or 'ineffable'. Then our being unable to imitate God would follow quite straightaway. After all, we cannot well fashion ourselves after that which lies beyond our ken. However, a non-imitative theology need not go that far. We could adopt a theology of analogy between God and us or even one where some terms we use about God are univocal with those we use about ourselves. In a non-imitative theology, we can acknowledge similarity between God and us, yet insist that there is no place for trying to be more God-like than we are, if we are. Non-imitative theology de-emphasizes the very mode of imitation as one informing the religious life.

The 'Divine Attributes'

To enunciate such a theology, let the 'Divine Attributes' be defined technically, though loosely, as those most associated, and uniquely so, with the classical concept of God. We would then include among the Divine Attributes those like God's being perfectly autonomous and self-sufficient, creating from nothing, being our ruler, having perfect power and perfect knowledge, being perfectly good, and living forever. These go with the classical concept of God.

According to non-imitative theology, God alone is perfectly autonomous.[21] We are not and should never strive in that direction. Not only do we depend upon God, we also depend upon each other and upon the cosmos in multiple and varied ways. Each of us is enmeshed in a structure of inter-being with the world. Realizing that autonomy is God's alone, no person would pretend to be free of an intimate consciousness of others, and each would be filled with gratitude to God and others for life and life's needs.

God alone creates from nothing, on the classical account. We do not. Our creative endeavors require materials, cooperation, and education and acculturation. Our creative abilities come to us from our ancestors and from their providing for us. No person should relate to creative achievement as though he or she produced it 'out of nothing'. Our debt to God and to others is great, and our creative achievements are ours only in that they come to light in and through us.

According to non-imitative theology, God alone is master. No person shall rule over another or over the world in the way God rules.[22] Any attempt by a human to do so is a human abuse of power. In the Jewish tradition, some have denigrated the institution of slavery because it is forbidden to subjugate oneself to anyone other than God. An example is the following rabbinical comment on Exodus 21. That chapter of the Bible deals with a man sold to slavery against his will, who then chooses to remain a slave and not go free when the obligatory time for servitude ends. He must then have his ear pierced (Babylonian Talmud, Tractate Kiddushin 22b).[23]

> How is the ear different from other parts of the body? [so that it is pierced rather than some other part of the body] The Holy One Blessed be He said: 'The ear which heard my voice at Mount Sinai when I said, "For it is to me that the Israelites are slaves": My slaves, and not slaves to slaves. And this one goes and chooses to remain with the master! Let [that ear] be pierced!'

This text does not condemn the institution of slavery. Rather, it condemns a person who wishes to remain a slave, freely submitting to human mastership. We should serve only God. Submitting willfully to a human master compromises our dedication to God's mastership. Here we can go further than this text, and in keeping with non-imitative theology contend that no person shall be *master* of another, since God alone is master. Just as God is called a 'master', so shall you *not* be a master. Of course this would apply to all human relationships.

According to non-imitative theology, God has perfect power. As such God alone can control events as God wishes. Human beings must realize that their control of events is limited and full control beyond their grasp. We should not be committed to the endeavor of total control over our own lives or the lives of others. We become human by learning to relax our hold on that dream of control. Even when praying to God for something we desire, we dare not attempt to appropriate God's control of affairs to our own ends, as though empowering ourselves with God's own power. We are not to insist on what we pray for, but leave it to God's will, that is, relinquish our own power to control the events of our lives.

According to non-imitative theology, God has perfect knowledge. Human beings must not think they do, either about everything or about a particular realm of knowledge. What we take to be our knowledge is fragmentary, proceeds haltingly, and is ever open to revision. Our knowledge is vulnerable to our weaknesses and fears. When we have much knowledge, we should not feel pride. For God's knowledge alone is perfect and not given to revision. Ours is always flawed.

God is perfectly good.[24] Humans are morally weak. Even the greatest of saints have lapses, temptations and doubts. We should elevate no person to the level of a God because of her or his apparent moral greatness. When we help to ease suffering we should be happy for what we have done, but not elevate ourselves to a moral pedestal. Only God stands on a moral pedestal. We can apply the non-imitative understanding even further by desisting from making over-all moral judgments of others entirely, refraining from classifying others as 'good' or 'bad' people. We may very well judge their actions, but only God gets judged as a person. God is good.

On non-imitative theology, God alone lives forever. A human being is born and dies. We are not God. When we try to play God and pretend we will live forever, we cause others and ourselves enormous suffering. In time, the sands will cover our most majestic monuments to ourselves, and all we now survey will become desolate. Only God will live. This is not a reason for despair, however. It is only a reason to decide to be human.

Non-imitative theology can be given either a non-realist or a realist construal. On the non-realist construal, within the religious life to say of a Divine Attribute, D, that God is or has D is to say that no person should try to embody D or pretend they are even close to achieving D. Statements about God have a normative intent only.[25] On the realist construal, within the religious life to say of a Divine Attribute, D, that God is or has D is to attribute D to God, to a reality possessed of independent existence. It is also to assert that no person should try to embody D or pretend they are even close to achieving D. Statements about God have both ontological and normative intent.

God has other attributes besides the 'Divine Attributes', as I defined them above. God acts mercifully, for example. So do we. On non-imitative theology, however, the emphasis would not be on our acting mercifully because God does, but on our being merciful because, for example, God wants us to be so. That God wants us to be so follows from the classical concept of God's moral goodness. In this way, non-imitative theology goes well with so-called 'divine command' or 'divine will' ethics.[26] An alternative motivation for acting mercifully would be because it is fitting and proper for a human being to do so.

There need be no difficulty figuring out which attributes we should not strive for in ourselves and which we should be embodying, though not imitatively. We require either a source of understanding of what God wills of us, or an awareness of the human condition to judge what is appropriate for us. By the principles of non-imitative theology itself, our understanding of such matters will be limited and open to revision.

Non-imitative theology should not secure its rationale by dwelling on human defects and limitations, and so basing itself on a disparagement of ourselves in comparison with God. Non-imitative theology should not be defeating of human confidence and daring. Quite the contrary. Non-imitative theology liberates, allows humans to be human, without feeling they fall short of God. Non-imitative theology does not create guilt or a sense of self-damnation.

Non-imitative theology stays neutral about the celebrated question whether God is transcendent or immanent, or on whether we have close relationships with God. God need not be thought of as far away. On non-imitative theology, God may be immanent, and may be found to permeate our everyday experience of others and ourselves. God may be the Eternal Thou, engaged in I-Thou intimacy with us. It's just that in non-imitative theology our appropriate responses to God will not include our desire to imitate God.[27]

Traditional religions contain strands apparently amiable to non-imitative theology. Rowan Williams finds voices in Christianity concerning the imitating of Christ, that direct the believer to an imitation of Jesus' humanity, in all of its vulnerability. In this strand of the tradition, 'the Spirit's work is to make the believer like Christ, and being like Christ means *living through* certain kinds of human experience – not once, but daily' (Williams, 1979, p. 7). 'The Christian,' writes Williams, 'meets pain in acceptance and *hope*; he or she confronts it, identifies with those experiencing it, and then struggles through it to grow into a new human-ness ... ' (p. 10).

The imitation of Jesus' humanity deflects us away from an *imitatio dei* of the sort my second proposal seeks to neutralize. I realize the problem for some feminists in the idea of the imitation of the man, Jesus. I offer this motif of Christian thinking, however, solely as a source for an emphasis in the spiritual life upon our humanity and its vulnerability, instead of an emphasis on being like God, as usually understood.

Williams finds in Irenaeus, especially, a concept of *imitatio dei* wherein 'the goal of Christian growth is a knowledge of God entirely founded in a sharing of life, an intimacy between persons, the fellowship of God with human beings *in their humanness*' (my emphasis) (Williams, p. 28). This sort of 'imitation' of God entails the capacity to share, as humans, in the divine life, by 'endurance and obedience'.[28]

In Rabbinic literature as well there seems to have been a secondary strand that would distance us from a theology of imitation. In a study of the concept of the image of God in Rabbinic literature, Yair Loberbaum has documented the tension between different schools of thought over the centrality of the image of God (Loberbaum, 1997). Loberbaum shows that the school of Hillel was committed to a theology of the image of God that motivates much of that school's legal decisions. However, the school of Shamai devaluated the notion, especially concerning the possibility of relating the human body to God's image, and according to Loberbaum deflated the significance of an 'image' theology in general (p. 176). Although pertaining directly to the image of God, this approach implies as a corollary a demotion of the idea of the imitation of God as well.

Further inquiry is needed to uncover possible additional alternative sub-traditions that would be congenial to non-imitative theology. In the meantime, I have noted those undercurrents favorable to a non-imitative theology of God that have come to my attention.

A common feminist protest against the classical concept of God portrays God's isolated, atomic splendor as a male ideal. On this view, men's psycho-development valorizes attaining atomic self-hood to break free from their initial identification with the feminine/mother (see Miller, 1976, and Chodorow, 1978). This contrasts with women's conception of the self, formed within the comfort of their early feminine identification with their mothers and not requiring a rupture from that self-definition. The emerging women's self remains embedded in a web of relationships, with no clear demarcation between herself and others. Accordingly, a God of autonomous isolation reifies, it may be charged, the male ideal self.

Non-imitative theology retains the classical concept of God's immaculate independence while meeting this feminist protest. We may say that 'just as God is a pristine, isolated, atomic self, so shall you *not* see yourself as such'. This follows from God's unique autonomy and self-sufficiency being one of the 'Divine Attributes', and so an attribute *not* to be copied. This aspect of non-imitative theology has been expressed in Hasidic literature by R. Kalonymus Kalman Epstein (d. 1823), who writes (*Maor Va'Shamesh*, 1842, 137b, my translation):

> If a person wishes to separate from the collective and to be alone in prayer or in any other homage to God, it will be impossible to attain the higher holiness ... For it is impossible for any creature to be solitary, only God, who is one, is solitary and unique ... that is why the Midrash says that God's holiness is higher than your holiness, for a person might think to be isolated in order to achieve holiness ... But that is only for God alone who is solitary and unique.

According to the above feminist psycho-developmental theory, non-imitative theology might be thought nevertheless to reflect a male desire for self-definition by difference and contrast, rather than by inclusion. If I think of myself as defined in opposition to God, am I not playing out once again a male need for self-definition by difference and isolation? The answer is that on the ground non-imitative theology need not function in that way at all. The understanding that we are to refrain from trying to be like God might not have required explicit mention were there not a history of *imitatio dei*. The non-imitation doctrine need be no more explicit to my thinking than my knowing that if I jump off a high roof I will likely die. At lunch-time, I wouldn't consider jumping off the top of my university building as a fast way to get to the street and the restaurant, but not because I will have worked through the reasons why this would not be a good idea. And I can live a non-imitative life without having to invoke non-imitative theology. We need not live with non-imitative theology before our eyes. Non-imitative theology is best served when imitative theology is simply forgotten from our considerations and decisions.

Non-imitative theology represents a radical departure from a feminist desire to have God as a model to be emulated for the flourishing of human spirituality and ideals. Nonetheless, non-imitative theology does not exclude our employing regulative models for human goodness and human flourishing. On the contrary, it is good and proper that we have such before our eyes. What I question is whether this has to be God. Instead, our models will be human, drawn from human life and history, and from religions and literature. Models may be multiple and diverse, some serving, say, economically underprivileged women, others serving, say, the affluent, academically trained. Let a polymorphous imaging of our greatest human spiritual potentials guide us under the all-encompassing unity of one concept of God.

Of course, the mere formulation of non-imitative theology would produce little social change. We would require its prominent espousal as well as the explicit joining of it to the ethical and political values that it enhances. In addition, non-imitative theology would have to find echoes in religious practice, rituals and texts, in order to have a serious influence on our lives.

I conclude, that social justice and human flourishing, therefore, do not require a radical change in the classical concept of God. The adoption of a non-imitative theology will do, providing a concept of God for all, women and men alike, enhancing human dignity, advancing human spirituality and furthering social justice.

Notes

1 For a good presentation of strong objectivity, see Anderson, 1998, pp. 76–83.
2 This seems to be Anderson's understanding of Richard Swinburne's approach to the philosophy of theism. See *ibid.*, Chapter One.
3 Recall that, in the 'classic' sense, 'God' names the eternal, all-powerful, all-knowing, and perfectly good, creator and sustainer of the universe. In the generic sense, 'God' names a reality, the mystical perception of which holds great meaning and value for subjects, and around which – God and the experiences – subjects find the focus and integration of their lives.
4 For forceful statements of this view, see Daly, 1973, and Hampson, 1990.
5 Anderson has been careful to distinguish between God as a regulative principle and God as a projection of our own subjectivity. See Anderson, 2000.
6 However, Hampson informs us there that she tends 'not to think of God as a "thou"'.
7 For a classical statement of libertarian feminism, see Frieden, 1974.
8 There are two tracks to Maimonides' approach to the doctrine. One track is that a person is like God in exercising the intellect. The more intellectual, the closer to being like God is a person. See Maimonides, *Guide of the Perplexed*, 1963, Part 1, Chapter 1. The second track is that a person is like God by embodying certain positive character-traits. I attend here to the second track alone. I am well aware of the problematic of the first track for feminist thought.
9 I do not mean to imply that Maimonides would be a friend of feminism.
10 My presentation here is necessarily sketchy and narrowly focused. For a fuller presentation, see Kreisel, 1994. See also Wurzburger, 1986.

11 Such a concept of God as 'the supreme being' has seemed to more than a few feminists to build a hierarchical dimension into the concept of God which then goes on to serve as a paradigm for men's hierarchical identification with God against women. However, as we shall see below, Maimonides' doctrine (officially at least) has the power to neutralize this shortcoming of that conception of God.

12 Notice that Maimonides says only that God 'is called' by certain terms not that God actually possesses these character traits. This is in keeping with Maimonides' regulative view of the matter. Maimonides here follows a rabbinic formulation found in *Sifre*. See Louis Finkelstein (ed.), 1969. In addition, some manuscripts of the Maimonides' text lack the word 'Him' in 'imitate Him'. This version suggests a further distancing from any idea of a real imitation of God.

13 Setel speaks of the Hebrew Bible in particular. But such issues carry over to the Christian Testament as well.

14 My translation. See Kasher, 1995, for an extensive discussion of Maimonides' interpretation of these verses. These verses are traditionally referred to as the 'thirteen attributes', but Kasher finds evidence that Maimonides would have counted only eleven, or fewer.

15 Elsewhere in the *Guide*, Part 3, Chapters 53–4, Maimonides limits the imitation of God to acting in loving kindness, in judgment and with righteousness. I suggest that these three summarize for Maimonides the attributes of the verses from Exodus.

16 These differences are mainly two: first, in the *Guide*, Maimonides seems to conceive of the imitation of God more in terms of types of *actions* to imitate rather than character traits to mimic. This difference is not critical to our present purposes. Secondly, in *Guide* Part 1, Chapter 54, Maimonides' discussion applies to the political ruler only. However, by the time Maimonides gets to Part 3, Chapters 53–4, this is generalized from the political to the ethical realm.

17 God's clothing the naked refers to Genesis **3**, where God provides clothing for Adam and Eve. God visits the sick in Genesis **18**, where God visits Abraham after circumcision. And, God's burying the dead refers to Deuteronomy **34**:6, which according to a rabbinic tradition recounts God's burial of Moses.

18 This is taken from the commentary of David Altschuler (eighteenth century), *Mezudat David*, to Job **40**:9.

19 I am greatly indebted in what follows to Berel Lerner, 1999.

20 See Feuerbach, 1957. For the shifts in Feuerbach's thinking over time, see Harvey, 1995.

21 Of course the notion of autonomy must be carefully fleshed out. For recent conceptions of autonomy, see O-Neill, 2000.

22 One human being may justly have power-over another if it is not absolute power and does not supposedly come from some intrinsic nature of the person holding the power. Examples of legitimate power-over are: the power an elected official has, the power of parents over children, and the power of an employer over an employee. God alone has absolute power that flows from God's intrinsic nature.

23 I am indebted for this example to Berel Lerner.

24 This component of the classical concept of God makes the current proposal vulnerable to the claim, endorsed by some feminists, as well as by others of course, that the evil of our world contradicts God's goodness. Some have argued that the very attempt to justify the world's evils shows hopeless callousness for the suffering victims of oppression. This is a controversial charge in philosophy of religion. I have discussed it in Gellman, 1997. For a good summary of the issues in the problem of evil, see Peterson, 1998. Missing in the present discussion is an attempt to work a solution of the problem of evil into the requirements of a successful non-imitative theology.

25 This non-realist analysis is due to Asa Kasher, 1983.

26 For the 'divine command theory', see Robert Adams, 1973, and Phillip Quinn, 1978 and 1990.

27 In this way, non-imitative theology is congenial to what David Hartman calls 'covenantal theology', according to which in a covenantal relationship God affirms our human integrity. See Hartman, 1985 and 2000.
28 I am thankful to Sarah Coakley for having brought Williams' approach to my attention.

Conclusion

We have found that the Argument from Perception is not universally rationally compelling, in the sense of rationally obligating all who would ponder
it. It does not compel four kinds of people:

1 Those who, because of God's non-dimensionality, will not grant recognition to a practice of identifying something as God in experience (per
   Chapter Three);
2 Those for whom supernatural explanation is not an explanatory option,
   and so will not countenance explaining an experience in terms of God's
   activity (per Chapter Four);
3 Those who rationally reject the Argument from Perception because of
   embracing an alternative explanation for God-perceptions (per Chapter
   Five); and
4 Those who, because of gender objections, will not accept the traditional
   context in which God-perceptions are explained to be of the classical
   God of theism, though this does not touch the generic concept of God
   (per Chapter Six).

On the other hand, none of the positions taken in (1)–(4) has been shown to
be rationally compelling for everyone either. Concerning (1), I have shown
in Chapter Three that a practice of identifying God in mystical experience
can be as acceptable as the practice of identifying physical objects in sense
perception. Therefore people can be in their rights to allow such a practice
to help shape their rational beliefs.

About (2), I have argued in Chapter Four against an attempt to disallow
supernatural explanation on conventionalist grounds. Further, the question
whether supernatural explanation can dwell together with our modern appreciation of science is contested, with philosophers taking positions on both
sides. Although I have not pursued the matter here, it would seem that one
could rationally argue for the recognition of supernatural explanation of mystical experiences of God within a scientific outlook. To help this synthesis
along I have presented the possibility that we could interpret God's activity in
mystical experiences of God in a non-interventionist mode, and thus make it
palatable to science. Furthermore, whether a purely naturalistic scientific
outlook is itself rationally compelling is likewise a contested issue.

Concerning (3), I have argued in Chapter Five that one would be more
inclined to accept an alternative explanation of mystical experiences of God

if one had independently dismissed the theistic explanation. One could be rationally justified in doing the latter if one or more of the arguments against God's existence convinced one. I have excluded the issue of arguments against God's existence from this study, so I leave open the possibility that one could show that God does not exist, thereby making alternative explanations of God-perceptions attractive. In any event, I have argued against some proposed alternative explanations, and have tried to show what it would take for a neuropsychological explanation to do the trick. If a person knows of such an explanation that works then they will possess good reason to deny the Argument from Perception.

On the other hand, there are also people who are justified theists. Perhaps after careful consideration they have concluded that one of the arguments for God's existence is convincing. Alternatively, perhaps they can justify their theism without any evidence in its favor. For them the issue of this book is not whether God-perceptions prove God's existence, but whether people know God, who exists, in mystical awareness. If this theist does not support (1) or (2), and either does not support (4) or accepts the generic concept of God, then I submit that, until coming face to face with a proven alternative explanation, the Argument from Perception is rationally compelling for them.

Regarding (4), I have tried to show in Chapter Six that we can retain the classical concept of God in the face of feminist concerns by modifying or demoting the notion of the imitation of God. If I am right, we can sustain the Argument from Perception. Furthermore, even if I am wrong, we can apply the argument at least to the generic concept of God.

So the Argument from Perception, together with the appropriate negations of (1)–(4), represents a line of reasoning that will be rationally compelling for some, though not for others.

Bibliography

Adams, Robert (1973), 'A Modified Divine Command Theory of Ethical Wrongness', in G. Outka and J.P. Reeder Jr. (eds), *Religion and Morality*, Garden City: Anchor, pp. 318–47.

Adams, Robert (1987), *The Virtue of Faith and Other Essays in Philosophical Theology*, New York: Oxford University Press.

Alcoff, Linda and Elizabeth Potter (eds) (1993), *Feminist Epistemologies*, New York: Routledge.

Allen, Amy (1998), 'Rethinking Power', *Hypatia*, **13**, 21–41.

Alston, William (1986), 'God's Action in the World', in Ernan McMullin (ed.), *Evolution and Creation*, Notre Dame: University of Notre Dame Press, pp. 197–220.

Alston, William (1991), *Perceiving God: The Epistemology of Religious Experience*, Ithaca: Cornell University.

Alston, William (1993), 'The Fulfillment of Promises as Evidence for Religious Belief', in Elizabeth S. Radclife and Carol J. White (eds), *Faith in Theory and Practice, Essays on Justifying Religious Belief*, Chicago and La Sale: Open Court, pp. 1–34.

Anderson, Pamela (1998), *A Feminist Philosophy of Religion*, Oxford: Blackwell.

Anderson, Pamela (2000), Review of Grace Jantzen, '*Becoming Divine*: Towards a Feminist Philosophy of Religion', *Theology and Sexuality: The Journal of the Centre for the Study of Christianity and Spirituality*, **13**, 121–5.

Aurbach, Efraim (1975), *The Sages, Their Concepts and Beliefs*, Jerusalem: Magnes Press.

Austin, James H. (1998), *Zen and the Brain*, Boston: MIT Press.

Bagger, Matthew C. (1999), *Religious Experience, Justification, and History*, Cambridge: Cambridge University Press.

Batson, C. Daniel, Patricia Schoenrade and W. Larry Ventis (1993), *Religion and the Individual, A Social-Psychological Perspective*, Oxford: Oxford University Press.

Bear, D. and P. Fedio (1977), 'Quantitative analysis in interictal behavior in temporal lobe epilepsy', *Archives of Neurology*, **34**, 454–67.

Beardsworth, Timothy (1977), *A Sense of Presence: The Phenomenology of Certain Kinds of Visionary and Ecstatic Experience, Based on a Thousand Contemporary First-hand Accounts*, Oxford: Oxford University Press.

Beer, Frances (1993), *Women and Mystical Experience in the Middle Ages*, Woodbridge: Boydell Press.

Bennett, Jonathan (1966), *Kant's Analytic*, Cambridge: Cambridge University Press.

Borchert, Bruno (1994), *Mysticism, Its History and Challenge*, York Beach, Maine: Samuel Weiser.

Brunn, Emilie Zum and Georgette Epiney-Burgard (1989), *Women Mystics in Medieval Europe*, trans. Sheila Hughes, New York: Paragon House.

Burnham, Sophy (1997), *The Ecstatic Journey: The Transforming Power of Mystical Experience*, New York: Ballantine.

Byrne, Peter (1995), 'Omnipotence, feminism, and God', *International Journal for Philosophy of Religion*, 37, 145–65.

Cardena, Etzel, Steven Jay Lynn and Stanley Krippner (eds) (2000), *Varieties of Anomalous Experience, Examining the Scientific Evidence*, Washington, D.C.: American Psychological Association.

Chodorow, Nancy (1978), *The Reproduction of Mothering: Psychoanalysis and the Sociology of Gender*, Berkeley: University of California Press.

Classen, Constance (1998), *The Color of Angels, Cosmology, Gender, and the Aesthetic Imagination*, London and New York: Routledge.

Coakley, Sarah (1996), 'Kenosis and subversion: on the repression of "vulnerability" in Christian feminist writing', in Daphne Hampson (ed.), *Swallowing a Fishbone? Feminist Theologians Debate Christianity*, London: SPCK, pp. 82–111.

Code, Lorraine (1991), *What Can She Know? Feminist Theory and the Construction of Knowledge*, Ithaca: Cornell University Press.

Colson, Elizabeth (1969), 'Spirit Possession among the Tonga of Zambia', in J. Beattie and J. Middleton (eds), *Spirit Mediumship and Society in Africa*, London: Routledge & Kegan Paul, pp. 69–103.

Cover, Jan (1999), 'Miracles and (Christian) theism', in Eleonore Stump and Michael J. Murray (eds), *Philosophy of Religion: The Big Questions*, Oxford: Blackwell, pp. 334–52.

Daly, Mary (1973), *Beyond God the Father, Toward A Philosophy of Women's Liberation*, Boston: Beacon Press.

Daly, Mary (1991), *Gyn/Ecology: The Metaethics of Radical Feminism*, London: The Women's Press.

d'Aquili, Eugene and Newberg, Andrew (1993), 'Religious and Mystical States: A Neuropsychological Model', *Zygon*, 28, 177–200.

d'Aquili, Eugene and Newberg, Andrew (1999), *The Mystical Mind: Probing the Biology of Religious Experience*, Minneapolis: Fortress Press.

d'Aquili, Eugene and Newberg, Andrew (2000), 'The neuropsychology of aesthetic, spiritual, and mystic states', *Zygon*, 35, 39–51.

David son of Joshua son of Abraham Maimonides (1997), *Instructor of Asceticism and Guide to Simplicity (Doctor ad Solitudinem et Ductor ad Simplicitatem)*, trans. P.B. Fenton, Jerusalem: Hevrat Meekitzeh Nirdamim.

Davis, Carolyn Franks (1989), *The Evidential Force of Religious Experience*, Oxford: Clarendon Press.

Delaney, Carol (1998), *Abraham on Trial, The Social Legacy of Biblical Myth*, Princeton: Princeton University Press.

Dewhurst, K. and A.W. Beard (1970), 'Sudden religious conversions in temporal lobe epilepsy', *British Journal of Psychiatry*, **117**, 497–507.

Elwood, Robert S. (1999), *Mysticism and Religion*, Second Edition, New York and London: Seven Bridges Press.

Etkes, Immanuel (1988), 'Hasidism as a Movement: The First Stage', in B. Safran (ed.), *Hasidism: Continuity or Innovation?*, Cambridge, Mass.: Harvard University Center for Jewish Studies, pp. 1–26.

Etkes, Immanuel (1996), 'The Study of Hasidism: Past Trends and New Directions', in Ada Rapaport-Albert (ed.), *Hasidism Reappraised*, London and Portland Ore.: Vallentine Mitchell, pp. 447–64.

Ettinger, Shmuel (1991), 'The Hasidic Movement – Reality and Ideals', in Gershon David Hundert (ed.), *Essential Papers on Hasidism*, New York: New York University Press, pp. 226–43.

Evans, Gareth (1980), 'Things Without the Mind – A Commentary upon Chapter Two of Strawson's *Individuals*', in Zak Van Straaten (ed.), *Philosophical Subjects, Essays Presented to P.F. Strawson*, Oxford: Clarendon Press.

Fales, Evan (1996a), 'Scientific explanations of mystical experiences, Part I: The Case of St Teresa', *Religious Studies*, **32**, 143–63.

Fales, Evan (1996b), 'Scientific explanations of mystical experiences', *Religious Studies*, **32**, 297–313.

Fales, Evan (2001), 'Do Mystics See God?' in Michael L. Peterson (ed.), *Contemporary Debates in the Philosophy of Religion*, Oxford: Blackwell.

Falk, Marcia (1986), 'And Hallow Them Both', *Journal of Feminist Studies in Religion*, **2**, 121–5.

Falk, Marcia (1996), *The Book of Blessings: New Jewish Prayers for Daily Life, the Sabbath, and the New Moon Festival*, Boston: Beacon Press.

Fenwick, P. (1996), 'The neurophysiology of religious experiences', in Dinesh Bhugra (ed.), *Psychiatry and Religion: Context, Consensus, and Controversies*, London: Routledge, pp. 167–77.

Feuerbach, Ludwig (1957), *The Essence of Christianity*, trans. George Eliot, New York: Harper.

Finkelstein, Louis (ed.) (1969), *Sifre* (Hebrew), New York: Jewish Theological Seminary, 1969, p. 114.

Frankenberry, Nancy (1998), 'Philosophy of religion in different voices', in Janet Kourany (ed.), *Philosophy in a Feminist Voice: Critiques and Reconstructions*, Princeton: Princeton University Press, pp. 173–203.

Frieden, Betty (1974), *The Feminist Mystique*, New York: Dell.

Gale, Richard (1994), 'Why Alston's mystical doxastic practice is subjective', *Philosophy and Phenomenological Research*, **54**, 869–75.

Gale, Richard (1995), *On the Nature and Existence of God*, Cambridge: Cambridge University Press.

Gellman, Jerome (1993), 'Religious diversity and the epistemic justification of religious belief', *Faith and Philosophy*, **10**, 345–64.

Gellman, Jerome (1994), 'Poetry of Spirituality', in D. Shatz and L. Kaplan (eds), *Rabbi Abraham Isaac Kook: Jewish Spirituality*, New York: New York University Press, pp. 88–119.

Gellman, Jerome (1997), *Experience of God and the Rationality of Theistic Belief*, Ithaca: Cornell University Press.

Gellman, Jerome (1998), 'On a sociological challenge to the veridicality of religious experience', *Religious Studies*, **34**, 235–51.

Geschwind, N. (1983), 'Interictal behavior changes in epilepsy', *Epilepsia*, Supplemental Volume **1**, 23–30.

Glouberman, M. (1975) 'Space and Analogy', *Mind*, **84**, 355–73.

Goiten, S.D. (1988), *A Mediterranean Society, Volume V, The Individual: Portrait of a Mediterranean Personality of the High Middle Ages as Reflected in the Cairo Geniza*, Berkeley, Los Angeles and London: University of California Press.

Goldenberg, Naomi (1979), *The Changing of the Gods*, Boston: Beacon Press.

Gross, Rita M. (1983), 'Steps toward feminine imagery of Deity in Jewish theology', in Susannah Heschel (ed.), *On Being a Jewish Feminist*, New York: Schocken Books, pp. 234–47.

Gross, Rita M. (1986), 'Roundtable discussion: Feminist reflections on separation and unity in Jewish theology', *Journal of Feminist Studies in Religion*, **2**, 127–30.

Haack, Susan (1993), *Evidence and Inquiry, Towards Reconstruction in Epistemology*, Oxford: Blackwell.

Hampson, Daphne (1990), *Theology and Feminism*, Oxford: Blackwell.

Hampson, Daphne (1996), *After Christianity*, Valley Forge, Pa.: Trinity Press.

Harding, Sandra (1991), *Whose Science? Whose Knowledge? Thinking from Women's Lives*, Ithaca: Cornell University Press.

Harding, Sandra (1993), 'Rethinking Standpoint Epistemology: What is "Strong Objectivity"?' in Linda Alcoff and Elizabeth Potter (eds), *Feminist Epistemologies*, New York: Routledge, pp. 49–82.

Hardy, Sir Alister (1980), *The Spiritual Nature of Man, A Study of Contemporary Religious Experience*, Oxford: Clarendon Press.

Hartman, David (1985), *A Living Covenant, The Innovative Spirit in Traditional Judaism*, New York and London: The Free Press.

Hartman, David (2000), *Israelis and the Jewish Tradition, An Ancient People Debating its Future*, New Haven and London: Yale University Press.

Harvey, Van A. (1995), *Feuerbach and the Interpretation of Religion*, Cambridge: Cambridge University Press.

Hay, D. (1979) 'Reports of religious experience by a group of post-graduate students: a pilot survey', *Journal for the Scientific Study of Religion*.

Helm, Paul (2000), 'Response to Gellman', in Paul Helm (ed.), *Referring to God, Jewish and Christian Philosophical and Theological Perspectives*, Richmond, Surrey: Curzon Press, pp. 90–94.

Hick, John (1989), *An Interpretation of Religion: Human Responses to the Transcendent*, New Haven: Yale University Press.

Horton, Robin (1993), *Patterns of Thought in Africa and the West*, Cambridge: Cambridge University Press.

Inge, W.R. (1899), *Christian Mysticism*, New York: Scribner's.

Irigary, Luce (1993), *Sexes and Genealogies*, trans. Gillian C. Gill, New York: Columbia University Press.

Ish-Shalom, Benyamin (1993), *Between Mysticism and Rationalism*, trans. Ora Wiskind-Elper, Albany: State University of New York Press.

Jacobs, Louis (1973), *Hasidic Prayer*, New York: Schoken Books.

Jacobs, Louis (1996), *Jewish Mystical Testimonies*, New York: Schocken Books.

James, William (1958), *The Varieties of Religious Experience*, New York: New American Library.

Jantzen, Grace M. (1988), *Julian of Norwich: Mystic and Theologian*, Mahwah, New Jersey: Paulist Press.

Jantzen, Grace M. (1989), 'Mysticism and experience', *Religious Studies*, **25**, 295–315.

Jantzen, Grace M. (1994), 'Feminists, philosophers, and mystics', *Hypatia*, **9**, 186–206.

Jantzen, Grace M. (1995), *Power, Gender, and Christian Mysticism*, Cambridge: Cambridge University Press.

Jones, Rufus M. (1914), *Spiritual Reformers in the 16th and 17th Centuries*, Boston: Beacon Press.

Kadushin, Max (1978), *Worship and Ethics: A Study in Rabbinic Judaism*, Westport, Conn.: Greenwood Press.

Kasher, Asa (1983), 'Minimal Judaism', *Jerusalem Quarterly*, **29**, 103–11.

Kasher, Hannah (1995), 'The commentary of Maimonides on the story of the cleft of the rock', (Hebrew) *Daat*, No. **35**, 29–66.

Kreisel, Howard (1994), '*Imitatio dei* in Maimonides' *Guide of the Perplexed*', *AJS Review*, **19**, 169–211.

Kuhn, Thomas S. (1962), *The Structure of Scientific Revolutions*, Chicago: University of Chicago Press.

Lakatos, Imre (1978a), *The Methodology of Scientific Research Programmes*, in John Worrall and Gregory Currie (eds), Cambridge and New York: Cambridge University Press.

Lakatos, Imre (1978b), *Philosophical Papers*, in John Worrall and Gregory Currie (eds), Cambridge and New York: Cambridge University Press.

Laughlin, Charles, John McManus and Eugene d'Aquili (1990), *Brain, Symbol, and Experience*, New York: Columbia University Press.

Lerner, Berel (1999), 'Oppressive Metaphor and the Liberating Literal Sense', in Ralph Bisschops and James Francis (eds), *Metaphor, Cannon and*

Community: Jewish, Christian, and Islamic Approaches, Bern: Peter Lang, pp. 233–41.

Levinson, Henry-Samuel and Malino, Jonathan (1999), 'Who's afraid of a BEE STING?' *Iyyun, The Jerusalem Philosophical Quarterly*, **48**, 293–326.

Lewis, I.M. (1986), *Religion in Context, Cults and Charisma*, Cambridge: Cambridge University Press.

Lewis, I.M. (1989), *Ecstatic Religion*, Second Edition, London: Routledge.

Loberbaum, Yair (1997), 'Imago Dei: Early Rabbinic Literature, Maimonides, and Nahmanides', unpublished PhD Thesis (Hebrew), Hebrew University.

M. (1964), *The Gospel of Ramakrishna*, trans. Swami Nikhilananda, Mylapore: Sri Ramakrishna Math.

MacQuarrie, John (1977), *Principles of Christian Theology*, 2nd edition, N.Y.: Scribners.

Maimonides, Moses (1963), *The Guide of the Perplexed*, trans. Shlomo Pines, Chicago: University of Chicago Press.

Martin, C.B. (1955), 'A religious way of knowing', in Antony Flew and Alisdaire MacIntyre (eds), *New Essays in Philosophical Theology*, London: SCM Press, pp. 76–95.

Martin, Michael (1990), *Atheism, A Philosophical Justification*, Philadelphia: Temple University Press.

Matt, Daniel C. (1990), '*Ayin*: The Concept of Nothingness in Jewish Mysticism', in Robert K.C. Forman (ed.), *The Problem of Pure Consciousness, Mysticism and Philosophy*, New York and London: Oxford University Press, pp. 121–59.

McGinn, Bernard (1991), *The Presence of God, A History of Western Christian Mysticism*, London: SCM Press.

Miller, Jean Baker (1976), *Toward a New Psychology of Women*, Boston: Beacon Press.

Nozick, Robert (1989), *The Examined Life: Philosophical Meditations*, New York: Simon and Schuster.

Oakes, Robert (1976), 'Biochemistry and theistic mysticism', *Sophia*, **15**, 10–16.

Ochshorn, Judith (1981), *The Female Experience and the Nature of the Divine*, Bloomington: Indiana University Press.

O-Neill, Onara (2000), *Bounds of Justice*, Cambridge: Cambridge University Press.

Ornstein, Robert Evan (1972), *The Psychology of Consciousness*, San Fransisco: W.H. Freeman.

Otto, Rudolf (1957), *The Idea of the Holy*, New York and Toronto: Oxford University Press.

Pagano, Robert R. and Stephen Warrenburg (1983), 'Meditation: In Search of a Unique Effect', in Richard J. Davidson, Gary E. Schwartz and David Shapiro (eds), *Consciousness and Self-Regulation*, **3**, pp. 153–210.

Pahnke, W. and W.A. Richards (1966), 'Implications of LSD and experimental mysticism', *Journal of Religion and Health*, **5**, 175–208.

Persinger, M.A. (1983), 'Religious and mystical experiences as artifacts of temporal lobe function: A general hypothesis', *Perceptual and Motor Skills*, **57**, 1255–62.

Persinger, M.A. (1984), 'Propensity to report paranormal experiences is correlated with temporal lobe signs', *Perceptual and Motor Skills*, **5**, 583–6.

Persinger, M.A. (1987), *Neuropsychological Bases of God Beliefs*, New York: Praeger.

Persinger, M.A. (1993), 'Transcendental meditation (tm) and general meditation are associated with enhanced complex partial epileptic-like signs: evidence for "cognitive" kindling?', *Perceptual and Motor Skills*, **76**, 80–82.

Peterson, Michael L. (1998), *God and Evil, An Introduction to the Issues*, Boulder and Oxford: Westview Press.

Phillips, D.Z. (1981), *The Concept of Prayer*, New York: Seabury Press.

Phillips, D.Z. (1988), *Faith after Foundationalism*, London and New York: Routledge.

Pike, Nelson (1992), *Mystic Union: An essay in the Phenomenology of Mysticism*, Ithaca: Cornell University Press.

Plantinga, Alvin (1979), 'Is belief in God rational?' in C. Delaney (ed.), *Rationality and Religious Belief*, Notre Dame: University of Notre Dame Press, pp. 7–27.

Plantinga, Alvin (1981), 'Is belief in God properly basic?' *Nous*, **15**, 41–51.

Plantinga, Alvin (1993), 'An evolutionary argument against naturalism', in Elizabeth S. Radcliffe and Carol J. White (eds), *Faith in Theory and Practice, Essays on Justifying Religious Belief*, Chicago and Lasalle: Open Court, pp. 35–65.

Pollock, John (1974), *Knowledge and Justification*, Princeton: Princeton University Press.

Quinn, Phillip (1978), *Divine Commands and Moral Requirements*, Oxford: Clarendon Press.

Quinn, Phillip (1990), 'The recent revival of divine command ethics', *Philosophy and Phenomenological Research*, **50** (Supplement), 345–65.

Rapaport-Albert, Ada (1996), 'Hasidism after 1772: Structural Continuity and Change', in Ada Rapaport-Albert (ed.), *Hasidism Reappraised*, London: Littman Library of Jewish Civilization, pp. 76–140.

Raphael, Melissa (1994), 'Feminism, constructivism, and numinous experience', *Religious Studies*, **30**, 511–26.

Rasmussan, Susan J. (1995), *Spirit Possession and Personhood Among the Kel Ewey Tuareg*, Cambridge: Cambridge University Press.

Roof, Wade Clark (1993), *A Generation of Seekers: The Spiritual Journeys of the Baby Boom Generation*, First Edition, San Francisco: Harper.

Roof, Wade Clark (1999), *Spiritual Marketplace: Baby Boomers and the Remaking of American Religion*, Princeton: Princeton University Press.

Rorty, Richard (1965), 'Mind-Body Identity, Privacy, and Categories', *Review of Metaphysics*, **19**, 24–54.

Rose, S. (1989), *The Conscious Brain*, New York: Paragon House.

Rosman, Moshe (1996), *Founder of Hasidism, A quest for the Historical Ba'al Shem Tov*, Berkeley: University of California Press.

Rowe, William (1982), 'Religious Experience and the Principle of Credulity', *International Journal for Philosophy of Religion*, **13**, 85–92.

Saiving Goldstein, Valerie (1992), 'The Human Situation: A Feminine View', in Carol P. Christ and Judith Plaskow (eds), *Womanspirit Rising: A Feminist Reader in Religion*, New York: Harper Collins, second edition 1992, pp. 25–42.

Schimmel, Annemarie (1978), *Mystical Dimensions of Islam*, Chapel Hill: University of North Carolina Press.

Sered, Susan Starr (1994), *Priestess, Mother, Sacred Sister, Religions Dominated by Women*, New York: Oxford University Press.

Setel, T. Drorah (1986), 'Roundtable discussion: Feminist reflections on separation and unity in Jewish theology', *Journal of Feminist Studies in Religion*, **2**, 113–18.

Strawson, P.F. (1964), *Individuals, An Essay in Descriptive Metaphysics*, London: Methuen Press.

Swinburne, Richard (1989), *Miracles*, New York: Macmillan.

Swinburne, Richard (1991), *The Existence of God*, Revised Edition, Oxford: Clarendon Press.

Swinburne, Richard (1996), *Is there a God?*, Oxford: Oxford University Press.

Teresa of Avila (1961), *Interior Castle*, ed. and trans. E. Allison Peers, Garden City, N.Y.: Doubleday.

Underhill, Evelyn (1945), *Mysticism, A Study in the Nature and Development of Man's Spiritual Consciousness*, London: Methuen.

Unger, Johan (1976), *On Religious Experience: A Psychological Study*, Uppsala: Uppsala University Press.

Wainwright, William (1981), *Mysticism, A study of its Nature, Cognitive Value, and Moral Implications*, Madison: University of Wisconsin Press.

Wallas, Graham (1926), *The Art of Thought*, New York: Harcourt.

Weeks, Andrew (1991), *Boehme: An Intellectual Biography of the Seventh-Century Philosopher and Mystic*, Albany: State University of New York Press.

Wexler, Philip (2000), *Mystical Society, An Emerging Vision*, Boulder: Westview Press.

Williams, Rowan (1979), *The Wound of Knowledge, Christian Spirituality from the New Testament to St John of the Cross*, London: Darton, Longman, and Todd.

Wulff, David M. (2000), 'Mystical Experience', in Etzel Cardena, Steven

Jay Lynn and Stanley Krippner (eds), *Varieties of Anomalous Experience: Examining the Scientific Evidence*, Washington: American Psychological Association, pp. 397–440.

Wurzburger, Walter (1986), '*Imitatio Dei* in Maimonides' *Sefer Hamitzvot* and the *Mishneh Torah*', in Jonathan Sacks (ed.), *Tradition and Transition: Essays Presented to Chief Rabbi Sir Immanuel Jakobovits to Celebrate Twenty Years in Office*, London: Jews' College Publications, pp. 321–4.

Wuthnow, Robert (1998), *After Heaven, Spirituality in America Since the 1950s*, Berkeley, Los Angeles and London: University of California Press.

Yandell, Keith (1993a), *The Epistemology of Religious Experience*, New York: Cambridge University Press.

Yandell, Keith (1999), *Philosophy of Religion, A Contemporary Introduction*, London and New York: Routledge.

Zagzebski, Linda (1996), *Virtues of the Mind: An Inquiry into the Nature of Virtue and the Ethical Foundations of Knowledge*, New York: Cambridge University Press.

Zeis, John (1999), Review of *Experience and the Rationality of Theistic Belief* by Jerome Gellman, *Faith and Philosophy*, **16**, 259–64.

Index